N E W   P L A Y S

MADAGASCAR

MAURITANIA

TOGO

Preface by
HENRY LOUIS GATES, JR.

UBU   REPERTORY   THEATER   PUBLICATIONS

Ubu Repertory Theater Publications
General Editors:
Françoise Kourilsky
Catherine Temerson
Kevin Duffy

Printed in the United States of America
Library of Congress Catalogue Card Number: 91-65893
ISBN: 0-913745-33-2

CONTENTS

PREFACE

Theater, Wole Soyinka argued in *Myth, Literature and the African World*, "is one arena, one of the earliest that we know of, in which man has attempted to come to terms with the spatial phenomenon of his being." Some form of theater seems common to almost every culture we know; but in a world of ever increasing cross-cultural exchange, we have seen multiple forms of theatricality developing alongside each other and, as frequently as not, intertwining. Plainly, modern African drama cannot be compartmentalized into such univocal categories as political satire, ritual theater, folk drama—as a glance at the diverse oeuvres of playwrights such as Jean Pliya, Jean-Baptiste Obama, or Bernard Dadié (to restrict myself to examples from francophone Africa) will attest. And yet Africa's playwrights have enjoyed liberal recourse to *all* these dramaturgic modalities. Such is the magic of *metissage* that amid the wealth of modern African literature, its crowning achievements may well be found in the realm of theater.

This realm has also been one of the most heavily policed, in part because its reach isn't restricted to those educated elites who are literate in European languages. Such a demotic appeal to the ruled makes its subversive potential of particular concern to the rulers; and, indeed, coercive structures of governance are prominently featured in all of these plays. But as I say, it would be as mistaken to view these works as ideological exercises merely as it would be to view them as verbal artifacts devoid of social content. Contemporary Africa presents itself in these pages with all its complexities and contradictions. But history is, too, a salient part of Africa's present—and not, as a character suggests in Moussa Diagana's compelling treatment of the legend of Wagadu, merely human refuse floating down a river. In dramatizing an episode of the historic empire of Ghana (which controlled a large area between the upper Niger and Senegal rivers), Moussa Diagana's play performs the function of so-called ritual drama everywhere, which is both to retrieve and to revise the legends that bind a people together, cement a common heritage, the imagined community that undergirds our contemporary identity. This he accomplishes not with pomp and portent, but sardonic humor and a sense of drama fueled by the rich verbal textures of griot and fool. This is not a story of kings and warriors: Moussa Diagana adopts the perspective of the heroine Sia Yatabere, and gives full weight to the concerns of hoi polloi, the commoners who too often are depicted merely as subjects, not agents, of their own history.

Charlotte-Arrisoa Rafenomanjato's "The Herd" finds an unlikely hero in Faly, who arouses the displeasure of the Chief when he suggests a communal effort to haul water back to a drought-stricken village. Forced to flee to the city, Faly has a difficult time adjusting to his new environment, where his acts of kindness are mistaken for acts of criminality. He can thus register both the advantages and the failings of urban modernity, the conflicting ways of life of town and country. It is clear, at any rate, where Rafenomanjato's own rather pastoral sentiments lie.

"The Crossroads," by Josué Kossi Efoui, foregrounds the techniques of dramaturgy through which it achieves its effects. A poet with a price on his head pursues love in an African police state of crossroads and roadblocks. The character's interactions are mediated by a prompter who knows the script of their lives, because it is his own life, too: "This play in my mind is my history," he confesses.

Jean-Luc Raharimanana and the other francophone playwrights in this volume have, no doubt, read and learned from the modernist achievements of Jean Genet, Jean Anouilh, Eugène Ionesco, Peter Weiss, and other dramatists from the European continent. And yet both form and substance are imbued with an over-whelming sense of the political exigencies of their own cultural locale. Thus "The Prophet and The President" reflects darkly upon the political madness that has overtaken too many neocolonial African states, using a technique that is expressive of a well-earned nihilism and despair.

Contrasting in every way, Sénouvo Agbota Zinsou's "Yevi's Adventures in Monsterland" evokes the ebullient world of the West African folktale. Bumptious Yevi, resourceful but reckless, may manage to escape the giants, but—being Yevi—he resolutely fails to learn the moral of the story, thus preparing him (and us) for an endless succession of misadventures to come. In a slightly more Brechtian vein, "The Singing Tortoise" features Podogan, corrupt civil servant and councilor to the king in a duel with his vainglorious son-in-law. No one will confuse this turtle with the Mutant Teenage

Ninja variety, but Sénouvo Agbota Zinsou has succeeded in producing a genuinely popular drama rooted in, but not confined to, one of West Africa's rich folkloric traditions.

In short, the plays collected in *Afrique II* amply demonstrate the range and diversity of contemporary African drama, their remarkable mixture of tradition and experimentation. Anyone familiar with the work of the Ubu Repertory Theater will understand the debt of gratitude we owe it, not only for encouraging the emergent creativity of successive generations of African dramatists, but for helping make their work available to a growing audience around the world.

HENRY LOUIS GATES, JR.

Sénouvo Agbota Zinsou was born in Lomé, Togo, in 1946. He continued his studies in France, receiving degrees in theater and communications. In 1968 he co-founded a university theater company, after working with several student companies, and began to be known outside Togo when his play *On joue la comédie* received first prize in Radio France Internationale's 1972 Inter-African Theater Competition. As part of the 1977 Festival of Black Arts and Culture in Lagos, Nigeria, he directed a production of the same play which later toured France. Since 1978, Zinsou has been director of the Troupe Nationale du Togo, a theater, ballet and music company. He directs the company in productions of his own plays, including *L'Arc en ciel* and *Le Club*. Zinsou premiered *La tortue qui chante* (*The Singing Tortoise*) in 1986 during the Francophone Summit in Lomé in a production that was later performed in France at the 1987 Limoges Festival. Zinsou is also a prize-winning short story writer, whose fiction and plays are published in France by Hatier.

Townsend Brewster was a playwright, librettist, lyricist, poet, translator, and critic. Three of his comedies, *Please Don't Cry and Say "No"*, *Arthur Ashe and I*, and *The Girl Beneath the Tulip Tree*, were produced Off-Broadway, as was his verse translation of Corneille's *Le Menteur*. Ubu commissioned many translations from him. These include Bernard Dadié's *Monsieur Thôgô-gnini*, available through Ubu Repertory Theater Publications, Maxime N'Debeka's *Equatorium*, included in Ubu's anthology *Afrique I*, and Sylvia Bemba's *Black Wedding Candles for Blessed Antigone*, included in Ubu's anthology *Theater and Politics*. He also translated Emmanuel Genvrin's *Etuves* and *Black Slavery*, which were given a staged reading at Hunter College Little Theatre as part of Ubu's 1989 festival "Homage to the Revolution." Brewster had just completed his translation of *Black Wedding Candles for Blessed Antigone* for Ubu at the time of his death, on February 1, 1990.

The premiere of the English translation of *The Singing Tortoise* was directed by Michi Jones at the David and Rae Aronow Theater at the City College of New York as part of the 1988 Ubu International Festival on March 17, 1988.

PROLOGUE

(*A noisy* CROWD *surrounds the* FOOL.)

FOOL: Silence! Silence! Ladies and gentlemen, the story is about to begin. (*Gradually, the* CROWD *quiets down*) Now listen carefully: There'll be no laughing. I'm telling a serious story. A tale told by an idiot, true enough, since its teller is the Fool. All the same, it's a story of life and death . . . I'll not dispute you if, at first, it sounds like a fable. But isn't it true that some of our fellow human beings, our countrymen, really belong in fables such as those about Anansi the Spider or the Tortoise? Consider my characters: To begin with, there's Agbo-Kpanzo, the hunter, the great hunter. What does he hunt? Lions, buffalo, elephants? Yes, but more than these, high-sounding titles, celebrity, fame. If he weren't a character in a fable, that is, if he lived in our time, he'd be the kind who gave you his card. He'd keep his name current in the newspapers, on the radio, on TV—even in the World of the Dead, if such a place exists. I'm sure you know the type.

(*reaction from the* CROWD)

Next, we have His Lordship, Podogan, Agbo-Kpanzo's father-in-law. The substantiality of his belly, the majesticness of his strut, even though he's not a king—at least, not yet—this substantiality, this strut tells the story. Now whatever you do, don't take him for your ordinary civil servant overfed and overeager to backbite, one who'll stop at nothing to claw his way to the top. No! His Lordship, Podogan, is merely a character in a fable. And, in the Land of Fables, he holds the rank of

4

The-King's Most-Trusted-Councilor—till recently, that is. In a word, His Lordship, Podogan, advised the King to pass a law mandating the death penalty for anyone who presumed to think, to dream, even, he might become king. Do you hear what I'm saying? As if such a thing could be! And, if such a thing could be, how does His Lordship know about it?

(*reaction*)

Well, now my story begins. You know the two leading characters. You need to know the King had decided to create a new position, the position of Chief Councilor. The Chief Councilor will have virtually complete control of the entire village and will be responsible, though on a regular basis, to only the King. Was it by accident that His Lordship put this idea into the King's head? But the King is cautious! His decision was to confer this position on the man his subjects loved the most. Neat, eh?

(*applause*)

Well, Agbo-Kpanzo, the great hunter, went into the great forest for the greatest hunt of his life, for enough game to feed the whole village. Isn't that a wonderful way to make yourself loved?

(*music*)

(*An unreal forest.* AGBO-KPANZO, *alone, speaks in an incantatory tone, with emphatic gestures, to the invisible spirits who fight against him.*)

AGBO-KPANZO: You know me, all of you! I'm Agbo-Kpanzo! Agbo-Kpanzo! Hey, hey hey, Agbo-Kpanzo! Agbo-Kpanzo never misses the mark. Agbo-Kpanzo never comes back empty-handed. Agbo-Kpanzo's not afraid of lions. Lions are afraid of Agbo-Kpanzo. Agbo-Kpanzo's not afraid of buffalo. Buffalo are afraid of Agbo-Kpanzo. Agbo-Kpanzo, hey, hey, hey, Agbo-Kpanzo! Spirit of the Forest, Spirits of the Winds, of the Rivers, of the Streams, and you, who are the soul power of the lion, the buffalo, the elephant, I know who's stirred you up against me. I know it's in the name of my enemy that you're playing these dirty tricks on me. For three days and three nights, I've been wandering through the forest without finding any game worthy of my prowess. And after I'd promised the village I'd bring back choice meat! I'd provide them a month of feasting! My enemy knows this. He knows, too, that, if I keep my promise, the whole village will sing my praises, and the King, perhaps, will appoint me to the much sought after position of Chief Councilor. So my enemy, who's my own father-in-law, has unleashed all the powers of the occult to bring about my humiliating failure, to make me come back empty-handed so the villagers, instead of with praise songs, will greet me with ridicule: "Today, the crocodile couldn't satisfy his stomach with even a shrimp." They'll go so far as to forget the mountains of meat I've brought them before. That's the way of the world.

But you've miscalculated, you demon spirits and you, my enemy, my dear father-in-law, who've called them up. Agbo-Kpanzo's going to win. I'm Agbo-Kpanzo, He-Who-Fears-Neither-The-Lion-Nor-The-Buffalo-Nor-The-Elephant! Even if I have to stay in this forest a week, a month, three months, I'm going to win.

(*A pause. Something moves just a few steps away from him.*) Ah, now I've got you! Don't move! You're a goner!

(*Whatever it is, moves.*)

A tortoise? All you are is a tortoise? A funny-looking tortoise? Are you really a tortoise, or are you someone disguised as a tortoise? Speak up! Lord help me, you look like a real tortoise! For starters, I'm going to kill you.

TORTOISE: Hey, don't shoot, Agbo-Kpanzo! First, listen to my song! Then decide whether or not you should kill me.

AGBO: What's this! A tortoise that not just talks but sings as well?

TORTOISE (*singing*): Trouble never troubles Man.
It's Man who troubles Trouble.

AGBO (*laughing*): Bravo! Bravo! Absolutely fascinating! With a little luck, you'll be a song star wherever you go when I'm done with you–Heaven or Hell. Not to be outdone, I have a song I'm going to sing for you.

(*singing*) Agbo-Kpanzo's not afraid of Trouble.
Trouble's afraid of Agbo-Kpanzo.
Hey, hey, hey, Agbo-Kpanzo!

TORTOISE: Yes, I know you're Agbo-Kpanzo. There is no need to keep yelling as if you're out to make the universe echo your name.

AGBO: Such nerve! Are you a devil or a sorcerer in disguise working for my father-in-law? That's it, right? That's why I'm going to kill you. So you can go tell them in the World of the Dead . . .

TORTOISE (*imitating him*): That I died at the hands of a great hunter named Agbo-Kpanzo. Ha, ha, ha!

AGBO (*annoyed*): You have good reason to laugh. I have better things to do than kill you.

TORTOISE (*laughing*): Of course, you have better things to do than kill me. You, Agbo-Kpanzo, are afraid to go back to the village empty-handed. You're afraid of the villagers' ridicule, of your wife's recriminations. Why she might even leave you. You're afraid of losing the popularity that could win you the position of Chief Councilor. You're afraid your enemy, your very own father-in-law, will beat you out.

AGBO: Stop! What you've just said to me, not a single human being has ever dared say. They know who I am.

8

TORTOISE: On the contrary, they don't know who you are. (*changing his tone*) But maybe I'll clue you in a little—if you'll behave yourself from here on in.

AGBO: I'm to let a tortoise clue me in? I see. I must take you back to the village so everyone will know . . .

TORTOISE: That Agbo-Kpanzo is a truly remarkable man. He brought back from the hunt a tortoise that not only speaks but sings, too. They'll talk about it everywhere, on the radio, on TV . . . Correction: by the backwater, in the market, in the fields, etc. And Agbo-Kpanzo, The-Man-Who-Brought-Back-The-Tortoise-That-Talks, will become even more famous.

AGBO: You've done enough talking. Now I'm going to put you on a leash.

TORTOISE: Hey, just a second, my friend. I haven't, as yet, stated the conditions under which I'll go with you.

AGBO: Beautiful! So you'll come with me only under certain conditions?

TORTOISE: Well, what did you think? You men are great for hasty decisions, but we tortoises are slow and steady. In other words, if you wish me to go with you of my own accord, there will be an absolute condition: You will never tell anyone that you've met or that you have in your possession a tortoise that sings and that speaks.

AGBO: On pain of death, you mean? I've heard that story before.

TORTOISE: All the same, I'll refresh your memory.

(*singing*) Trouble never troubles Man.
It's Man who troubles Trouble.

SCENE II

(AGBO-KPANZO'S *hut*)

NYOMADU: Where's the meat?

AGBO: Have a little patience, dear. When I've told you of my adventures, you'll see once again that your husband, Agbo-Kpanzo . . .

NYOMADU (*interrupting him*): Is a remarkable man, right? Where's the meat? Agbo, where's the meat?

AGBO: Let me explain. At one point, I was chasing a formidably ferocious wild boar . . .

NYOMADU: I've already heard your wild-boar story at least a hundred times these ten years. If you have any meat, give it here! (*shouting*) I'm hungry, I tell you! Where's the meat?

AGBO: Some people start the second they're a little bit hungry.

NYOMADU: Spare me the news that I'm one of them. Have you brought back any game, yes or no?

AGBO: You'll have plenty of game, dear.

NYOMADU: Good! As I thought, you're making game of me. I'm going to my father's for dinner.

AGBO: No, Nyomadu. I know your father. To get the position of Chief Councilor, he'd stop at nothing.

He'd even spread the ridiculous rumor that Agbo-Kpanzo had sunk to not being capable of feeding his wife.

(*calling after her*) Wait! Look, I brought something for you.

NYOMADU (*astounded*): A tortoise? And it's a good big one, too. Why have you seen fit to keep me waiting?

AGBO: Listen carefully. This tortoise is special.

NYOMADU: It does something unusual, does it?

AGBO: Unusual? I'd say so. (NYOMADU *begins to laugh.*) Don't laugh. I'm serious.

NYOMADU: Well, what does it do? Dance? Sing?

AGBO: Exactly, it sings. Even better, it speaks. And what remarkable things it says!

NYOMADU (*laughing*): Remarkable!

AGBO: It's no laughing matter. This is no real tortoise. It's a demon in disguise, and I've brought it back only after—

NYOMADU: A frantic, furious life-and-death struggle.

AGBO: I swear I went for three days and three nights without eating, without drinking, without sleep—

NYOMADU: You fought with the demons and the spirits of the forest. You vanquished them all. You brought them low. One of them managed to turn himself into a tortoise. You captured him and brought him back alive. Bravo! As for me, well now I'm going to change him into a good mess of fritters.

AGBO: Don't touch it! Wait, Nyomadu! The least I should do is let you hear its song. Listen.

NYOMADU: I'll listen while it sings from the bottom of the stewpot.

AGBO: It sings, I tell you. Just wait. Sing, tortoise, sing. Don't you see my wife has the ax poised over your head, and she's ready to butcher you? Are you trying to show me you're not afraid of dying? I'm begging you, sing!

NYOMADU: That did it! I've heard enough! I'm going to my father's. Good-bye! (*She exits.*)

AGBO (*in desperation*): Don't go! Don't go! Nyomadu! I assure you it can sing. It's going to sing . . . She's gone to her father's. Why wouldn't you sing? Why wouldn't you sing?

TORTOISE (*singing*): Trouble never troubles Man.
It's Man who troubles Trouble.

FOOL (*surrounded by the* CROWD): Yes, he's here! The one you've all been waiting for! The great, the mighty, the redoubtable Agbo-Kpanzo!

(*applause*)

Now tell me how many fools are there in this village at this point in time? Of course, the first on the list is easy. It's yours truly.

(*laughter*)

No comment. But the second? Who can it be? Who? Who? Well, I'm going to tell you. It's the man who makes tortoises sing.

(*silence*)

Ah, my answer intrigues you. Who fits that description? You all know him. It's the great, the mighty, the remarkable Agbo-Kpanzo. Yes, that same gentleman who's joining us now.

AGBO: What are you blabbering about? What have I ever done to you, hunchback, to make you insult me?

FOOL: I'm not insulting you, dear friend and colleague.

AGBO: Colleague?

FOOL: You and I, we're both fools. The people think being crazy is a pitiful state. But I say it's not, especially now that the King is in the market for a Chief Councilor. (*He bursts out laughing.*) From his

14

latest journey to Wonderland, my friend and colleague has brought us back a marvelous, a miraculous–tortoise.

AGBO: Hunchback!

FOOL: A tortoise the size of two huts end-to-end . . . and . . . and . . . that sings!

AGBO (*attacking the* FOOL): Quiet! Or I'll throttle you! Get out of here! Get out of here right now!

FOOL: Certainly, I'll get out of here. But bear in mind that, unlike everyone else, I won't get out before I've told the truth.

Scene IV

AGBO (*whispering*): You just saw how the Fool insulted and ridiculed me. I'm Agbo-Kpanzo, and a fool insulted me!

TORTOISE (*singing*): Trouble never troubles Man.
It's Man who troubles Trouble.

AGBO: Oh, so now you decide to sing! You waited till after my wife has left me. You waited till after my father-in-law has spread false rumors about me. He's saying I brought back a tortoise that's a witch, and that it devoured Koffi's child and Kossi's mother. And now he's summoned me to his home. To get the position of Chief Councilor, he'll stop at nothing.

TORTOISE (*singing*): Trouble . . .

AGBO: Give me a break. Especially since everything that's happened to me is all your fault. Don't mention "Trouble" to me. You're Trouble personified.

TORTOISE: I gave you fair warning. So from now on, watch out.

AGBO: What do you mean this time?

TORTOISE: I mean, when you go to your father-in-law's, watch out. Otherwise, trouble . . .

AGBO: Trouble, trouble. That's the only word that ever comes out of your mouth.

TORTOISE (*laughing*): Could it be you're getting superstitious? (*pause*) Do you need a magic spell to take with you to your father-in-law's?

AGBO: Your magic spell's a joke, and so are you. I, Agbo-Kpanzo, am not afraid of anything. (*He starts off and then comes back.*) This magic spell, what is it exactly?

TORTOISE: But you're not afraid of anything.

AGBO: Tell me about it anyway. You never know.

TORTOISE: Okay. The liar digs a pit for others but falls into it himself.

AGBO (*repeating the* TORTOISE's *words*): The liar digs a pit for others but falls into it himself. (*After a while, he laughs.*)

Scene V

(PODOGAN and two of his WITNESSES are preparing themselves "spiritually" to receive AGBO-KPANZO by means of a fetish ritual. Enter AGBO-KPANZO. The WITNESSES hide.)

PODOGAN: Agbo-Kpanzo, I want the truth. Because now, this business has gone too far. The whole village is topsy-turvy. The only thing they talk about is your tortoise. I understand your desire to become a celebrity, to make yourself popular so you'll get the position of Chief Councilor. But maybe you haven't chosen the surest road to success. You're too young; you make blunders. Blunders you're bound to regret, eh?

(pause)

As of now, the King isn't saying anything. But, if he's not saying anything, it means he's biding his time. As a minister privy to his secrets, I know whereof I speak. In a word, the King has asked me, as both His-Most-Trusted-Councilor and your father-in-law, to have my daughter spy on you. And what she says about you is mind-boggling! I'd like to do something to save your life . . . But, I warn you, lying doesn't sit well with me. So, the truth, and be quick about it! Who are your accomplices?

AGBO: My . . . what?

PODOGAN: I clearly said, "your accomplices." If I say, "your accomplices," it's because I know they exist.

AGBO: That who exist?

18

PODOGAN: Those you cooked up this scheme with.

AGBO (*laughing*): Anything for a laugh.

PODOGAN: Anything for a laugh? I, Podogan? Take a good look at me. Could anyone see this face and laugh? (AGBO-KPANZO *bursts out laughing.*) Don't you know I'm bad medicine?

AGBO: That's something everybody knows.

PODOGAN: You dare say that to me? Then I no longer look on you as my son-in-law. But rather as an enemy of the King. And I'll go ahead and make my report. I'll tell him you're the spirit behind the plot.

TORTOISE (*singing offstage*): Trouble never troubles Man.

PODOGAN: Who's that? Oh, but it can't . . . it can't . . . it can't be. The voice of the Tortoise! The, then, then, it's true? Come here, little tortoise, come here. You see, Agbo, I also have a singing tortoise. You're not the only one it seems. And mine has greater powers than yours. You planned to use your tortoise to get the position of Chief Councilor? Is that it? And, all along, I've had the same kind of tortoise for more than thirty years. I keep it in my bedroom—as both discretion and modesty require. By means of this tortoise, I discover, denounce, defuse all the enemies of my King and my village. I hope you see, Agbo, that your magic tortoise isn't a patch of mine. If that's what you've been counting on to get the position of Chief Councilor, forget it.

AGBO (*having grown more and more impatient*): The liar digs a pit for others but falls into it himself.

PODOGAN: What? What's that you're muttering? Something about making someone fall?

AGBO: Where is your tortoise, then?

PODOGAN: You mean you don't see my tortoise? You don't see that tortoise that's right in front of your eyes? That tortoise that sang just now?

AGBO: Very funny.

PODOGAN: Very funny? As I've told you, I'm always dead serious.

AGBO: Except for this time since this tortoise is mine.

PODOGAN: How's that? What did you say?

AGBO: You heard me. This tortoise is mine.

PODOGAN: No! It can't be possible! What's the world coming to? I've never seen mankind so vicious. Oh, what evil times! For gain, for a high place in society, a man will steal, will cheat even his own father-in-law, is that it? From the way things are developing, I shouldn't be surprised if soon everyone stood ready to ensnare his own parents, chop them into bits, and cook them on spits to sell in the market. "Shish kebabs of human flesh, twenty-five francs apiece!"

AGBO (*aside*): The liar digs a pit for others but falls into it himself.

PODOGAN: Great. Now you're talking about digging a pit for me.

AGBO: Listen, father-in-law, if that tortoise appeals to you, since I've been looking for a way to get rid of it anyway, take it.

PODOGAN: So, my boy, you're trying to pull a fast one, eh? You're saying all this so I'll tell my daughter to go back to you, and then, when you and she have settled your differences, you'll come yelling to me, "Give me back my tortoise! Give me back my tortoise!" No, next to me, you're a slowpoke. I refuse your gift. Your spurious gift. That tortoise is mine. And that's that. Besides, when have you ever given me anything? Well, have you ever since the beginning of time? The dowry? What definite proof do you have of my taking your dowry? Huh? You're about to mention the witnesses? But who are these witnesses? Anyone in the world can dig up phony witnesses. All he has to do is bribe them. No? You don't believe me? Me, Podogan, the King's-Most-Trusted Councilor? Well, I'm going to dig up my own witnesses here and now, honest witnesses who'll settle the matter once and for all. (*He exits.*)

TORTOISE (*singing*): Trouble . . .

AGBO (*to the* TORTOISE): You! You've followed me to stir up more trouble.

TORTOISE: Possibly so. But also possibly because, from living with you, I've come to feel a certain concern for you. In any event, isn't the formula working? The liar digs a pit for others . . .

(PODOGAN *enters with his* WITNESSES *and his daughter,* NYOMADU.)

FIRST WITNESS (*to* PODOGAN): Fifty!

PODOGAN (*softly to the* THREE WITNESSES): Forty. And that's my final offer. (*aloud for* AGBO-KPANZO's *benefit*) My good friends, do you recognize this tortoise?

WITNESSES: Yes.

PODOGAN: Whose is it?

WITNESSES: Yours, Your Lordship.

PODOGAN: Since when?

FIRST WITNESS: Well, . . . for the past fifty years. (*With a look,* PODOGAN *indicates no.*)

SECOND WITNESS: More like forty.

THIRD WITNESS: Let's say somewhere between sixty and forty.

AGBO: The liar digs a pit for others . . .

PODOGAN: If those are magic words you're repeating, I'll have you know they won't work against me.

(*At a sign from* PODOGAN, *the three* WITNESSES *take out little bells, ringing them as they utter indistinguishable mumbo-jumbo.*)

AGBO: And are you done with this farce now?

WITNESSES: Farce? What farce?

PODOGAN (*pointing to* AGBO-KPANZO): He tried to steal my tortoise. I caught him red-handed here in my own hut. It's a prison offense, but I'm strong for family ties, no matter what, not to mention family honor. It would take more than a mere tortoise to make me send my son-in-law to jail, thereby tarnishing the reputation of a man like Agbo-Kpanzo. It's a shame all the same. You take a man to be honest, noble . . . and, then, one day, you find out he's a thief.

NYOMADU: Agbo, haven't you anything to say to my father?

AGBO: What do you want me to say to your clown of a father?

PODOGAN: Now I'm a clown! First, you rob me; then you call me names! It's too much! Starting today, between you and my daughter . . .

NYOMADU: May I have a word with you, Father?

PODOGAN: Speak out, Daughter, speak out to confound this robber; speak to defend the honor of your outraged father.

NYOMADU: Father, I recognize this tortoise . . .

PODOGAN: You say you recognize it, Daughter? Here's yet another witness to neutralize this bandit's evil. Speak, Daughter.

NYOMADU: I mean to speak the truth, Father.

PODOGAN: Speak the truth, Daughter. You couldn't lie when you father's interests are at stake.

NYOMADU: The truth of the matter . . .

PODOGAN: Is that you recognize this tortoise as mine, don't you?

NYOMADU: This tortoise is the one that Agbo . . .

PODOGAN (*at the top of his voice*): Stole! Stole from me! Say it!

NYOMADU: No. It's the one he brought back from the forest.

PODOGAN (*After a pause, he screams.*): Iyiyiyiyiyi! The world's gone completely rotten ! My own daughter! I was right to say that children would soon sell their own parents as shish-kebabs. My own daughter is in on the plot whipped up against me. My own daughter! (*He sheds crocodile tears.*) No! In such times, it would be better not to live!

NYOMADU: Listen, Father. That's just an ordinary tortoise. I can personally guarantee you it doesn't sing.

PODOGAN: But I heard it, myself, just a while ago . . . What am I saying? I've heard it sing every day for the thirty years I've owned it.

NYOMADU: Fine. If what you're saying is true, make it sing now. That way, I'll know it's not the same as Agbo-Kpanzo's.

PODOGAN: That won't be hard. I'll just tell it to . . . (*with embarrassment after a pause*) What's its name? Toto? . . . Tutu? . . . Titi? All right, come on, darling, my little baby, sing for your sister, Nyomadu. Sing sweetly, and I'll give you . . . Now, what does it eat? I'll give you a big chunk of charcoal. (*He sees that* AGBO-KPANZO *is laughing.*) Agbo-Kpanzo, what are you laughing at? Ah, I see, you've cast a spell on my tortoise, and it can't sing anymore. You won't get away with it. You're going to make it sing this instant, or else I'll take terrible revenge. Make the tortoise sing, Agbo-Kpanzo.

AGBO: Take my word for it, father-in-law, the tortoise sings but never on command.

PODOGAN: I wouldn't take your word for a thing. You cast a spell on my tortoise. You've snatched its voice away. You're going to give it back, and my tortoise is

25

going to sing. Or else! I'm going to count to ten. If the tortoise doesn't sing, the King will learn . . . the truth. Heads will roll. (*As* PODOGAN *counts,* AGBO-KPANZO *laughs uproariously.*)

SCENE VI

FOOL (*surrounded by a noisy* CROWD): Listen! Listen! The hump on my back is still filled with stories! Brand new and true stories! A tortoise that sings, it's worth a fortune to someone who knows how to use it. Even without getting to be Chief Councilor, its owner can grow rich; it's all in how you put the story over. That's why man invented public relations, propaganda, slogans. If, for example, he advertises the tortoise as a cure-all that turns barren women fruitful, impotent men virile, that guarantees love, luck, lucre, everyone will line up at the door of Podogan, His Lordship of the Singing Tortoise—since he's the one who has his hands on it. Except it seems His Lordship has a serious problem. The Tortoise has stopped singing. Podogan believes Agbo-Kpanzo knows the secret of making it sing. Now, as you know, according to His Lordship, His Lordship can do anything. What does a fool make of this? There are now three fools in the village, myself, Agbo-Kpanzo, and that most inscrutable fisher in troubled waters, His Lordship Podogan.

(*music*)

Podogan (*hypocritically*): Agbo, forget about this little
rivalry between us over the position of Chief Councilor. If you want it all that much, I'll let you have it.
The Civil Service isn't profitable. I'm thinking of
going into private practice, actually. But there is one
thing worrying me now, and that's your magic spell. I
must know how to break it. Daughter, you tell him
too.

Nyomadu: You heard him, Agbo. He must know how to
break your magic spell.

Agbo: And what magic spell is this?

Podogan (*falsely affable*): Listen, Agbo. My daughter's
the tie that binds you and me together. If I turn in a
bad report to the King, that will be the end of you.
And, if it's the end of you, it's my own daughter who'll
be the widow. Therefore, since my primary duty is to
the family, you and I must come to an understanding.
We each must make a choice: You, between your
magic spell and your wife, I, between my daughter
and my King. My decision, you already know. The
Civil Service isn't profitable. A high-ranking position
with the King is a justifiable aim, but be warned by my
thirty years of experience at Court, which have taught
me no one can ever be sure of keeping in the King's
good graces. A disturbing dream, a bad mood, an
unpropitious oracle, an out-and-out lie, a mere suspi-
cion, and you're sacked—even more, arrested and
sent to jail. You listen to the radio regularly, don't
you? "So-and So has been stripped of his office." Ah,

yes, I, Podogan, as of now, am still hanging on . . .
It's because I know the ropes. And, if I do say so,
myself, I don't miss a trick. You'd never be able to
bring it off. You've got to know how to anticipate, test
for, select, and come up with on cue, according to the
time, the place, and the situation; the precisely proper
word; if you can't, you've no hope of constantly
keeping in the King's favor. Such work requires
tremendous subtlety, energy, vigilance, and percep-
tion, none of which you, as yet, have been able to
come by, my boy. People see my job as all sleaze and
slander. They don't know what it costs me, what
sacrifices I make . . . for my native village. All well
and good. Right now, I'm still in the King's good
books. But who knows what may happen tomorrow?
No, Agbo, the family's the only thing that lasts. Here
and now, just as we are, aren't my daughter, you, and
I perfectly happy? Aren't we? No, I'm not going to
risk this happiness for a measly position at Court. So,
Agbo, reveal the magic spell, and bring this story to its
happy ending.

AGBO: Father-in-law, I repeat there's no magic word
that makes the tortoise sing.

PODOGAN (*angrily*): There's no magic word! Do you take
me for a child? I know more about magic than you do.
So I know there's no magic without a spell.

AGBO: There's nothing magic about the tortoise.

PODOGAN: Then how do you send it to rob and murder
your victims? You think I'm not in the know? You're

Scene VIII

NYOMADU: Father, are you really going to make this report to the King?

PODOGAN: And what else would you have me do since he won't reveal the magic spell? Suppose I appear before the King to give an account of this tortoise business. If my report is complete, an assignment carried out to the letter, he'll be pleased; he'll congratulate me; I'll be one step ahead of my colleagues on the Privy Council, and perhaps I'll get the position. But, if, on the contrary, the King asks me, "Does this tortoise really sing?" and I stammer and stutter, . . . Can you picture me stammering and stuttering to the King? No, I'd be running the risk of losing not only my chance of promotion but my present post as well. Since Agbo-Kpanzo knows as much, he's not revealing the magic spell on purpose. It's not enough for him to beat me out as Chief Councilor. No, Agbo's plotting my downfall. But I'm smarter and stronger than he is.

NYOMADU: Father, you're getting all upset over nothing. Agbo's not plotting against you.

PODOGAN: Agbo's not plotting against me? You're making me believe that you're in on it.

NYOMADU: You can't believe I'm in on it.

PODOGAN: Oh, no? Nothing's impossible. Nowadays, you can't assume anyone's innocent. What does it mean to be innocent? Not that you've done no evil. But rather that, having committed the most heinous crime in the world, you're clever enough or have enough clout, money, connections to come up smelling like a rose. Now, I've always been innocent and I always shall be, despite my enemies and their hanky-panky.

NYOMADU: Father . . .

PODOGAN: Listen, if you're really my daughter, go see your crook of a husband and persuade him to reveal the magic spell by tomorrow. Otherwise, I'll be fiendish first and innocent later.

NYOMADU: I'm going!

(THE WITNESSES *enter.*)

PODOGAN: Well, what's the latest?

FIRST WITNESS: Everything's going well. Public opinion's coming closer and closer to deciding in your favor.

SECOND WITNESS: But don't get too confident. Our Fool is talking rather too loudly against you. It's a bit unsettling.

PODOGAN: Yes, to a certain extent, it's unsettling. Go find our Fool and bring him here to me. (THE WITNESSES *exit.* PODOGAN *approaches the* TORTOISE, *sighs, and addresses it.*)

If only you'd sing! You're here; you're listening, I

know, and you're aware of my problem. Yet you no longer sing. Come on, sing! Sing! What's the magic spell for changing yourself into a tortoise, huh? (*pause*) Now, listen here, Mr. Man-Pretending-To-Be-A-Tortoise, I'm not playing. I wasn't born yesterday. I've seen your type before. Men who've changed themselves into snakes, cats, owls in order to eat their fellow men up or commit other atrocious crimes. I've tracked them down and destroyed them. You'd better realize with whom you're dealing. I'll give you one more chance. Who are your accomplices? You're going to tough it out? Well, I'm tough, too. And hard as nails. I'm sure you've heard of Podogan's special way of torturing prisoners. Don't think your shell will protect you. I'm quite capable of ripping off your shell with my bare hands. (*He jumps on the* TORTOISE *and vainly tries to tear off its shell. Out of breath, he falls to the floor exhausted.*) Well, are you going to sing? Are you going to sing? All right, then, take the consequences. Tomorrow, when I hand in my report, to the King, I'll wipe you out! You and all the other phony tortoises like you! You'll all go to the gallows with your ringleader Agbo-Kpanzo!

SCENE IX

PODOGAN: Is it true you do nothing but speak against me?

FOOL: As His Lordship, Podogan knows, The Fool never speaks against anyone. He merely reports what goes on around him.

PODOGAN: You gentlemen of the press . . .

FOOL: Gentlemen of the press? Who?

PODOGAN: Now don't try to be sly. It amounts to the same thing, doesn't it? Now, if I've sent for you, it's to do you a good turn. (*taking out money*) What would you think of something in the neighborhood of, say, a hundred cowry shells?

FOOL: It's a nice neighborhood.

PODOGAN: Then, this money's all yours. (*He gives him the money.*) Its purpose is to end your speaking evil of me. You'll have a hundred more if you can . . . help me defeat my enemies.

FOOL: Does His Lordship, Podogan, have enemies?

PODOGAN: Do you mean to tell me you don't know Agbo-Kpanzo and his gang are out to get me?

FOOL: Why are they out to get you?

PODOGAN: How do I know? Possibly because of the position of Chief Councilor.

34

FOOL: Chief Councilor! They're way too puny! That's a job for you.

PODOGAN: A job for me, you say?

FOOL: Yes, that and more.

PODOGAN: More? What do you mean, "more"?

FOOL: "More" means the throne. Your Lordship's presence impresses me greatly. When I see you passing by, I say to myself, "Podogan should be King." When you strut, I seem to hear the griot's drum booming as he sings your praises in time with each of your steps. When I see you sitting down, I imagine a multitude of courtiers around you each one groveling to prove he's more loyal, more devoted than the next man. When you smile, they smile; when you're sad, they sadden. I hear in the street, on the public squares, everywhere, I hear thousands of voices singing It's His Lordship, Podogan. But it should be His Highness, Podogan. Long Live King Podogan the First!

PODOGAN (*as if in ecstasy at the* FOOL's *words*): Long live King Podogan the First! (*He catches himself.*) What you've just said is a serious offense. If you weren't a fool I'd clap you into jail.

FOOL: Jail? For what?

PODOGAN: The law prohibits anyone from dreaming he's King.

35

FOOL: Which of us dreamed he was King?

PODOGAN (*embarrassed*): Er . . . Er . . . Good point . . . You'll have a hundred cowry shells and much more, Fool, if you'll work for me.

FOOL: What must I do?

PODOGAN: You hold great sway over public opinion . . . as you know perfectly well. To begin with, use it to make everyone, including the King, if possible, believe that Agbo-Kpanzo and his gang are criminals who, in the guise of tortoises, commit felonies. You might add they're plotting against the King.

FOOL: Anything else?

PODOGAN: Yes. If you bring it off, you'll get lots of cowry shells.

FOOL: Fine. Long live King Podogan the First!

PODOGAN: Be still, you lame-brain! That's for later.

FOOL (*shouting*): Long live King Podogan the First!

PODOGAN: But you mustn't yell like that. Someone will hear you.

FOOL (*louder than ever*): Long live King Podogan the First!

PODOGAN: You . . . you're going to get me into trouble.

FOOL (*louder still while beating a drum*): Long live King Podogan the First!

PODOGAN: This lunatic will ruin me. I'm beginning to suspect he's a member of the gang.

Scene X

(The CROWD, *wanting to hear the latest news, follows the* FOOL.)

CROWD: The news! The news! The latest news!

FOOL: Okay. The news, I'll make it brief because I'm in a hurry today, and, like me, every one of you wants this tortoise story to end as soon as possible. Here goes: For two days, Podogan plagues his daughter to get her husband to reveal that magic spell that makes the Tortoise sing. But Agbo-Kpanzo keeps on insisting there's no magic spell. So Podogan, abusing his power as village police chief, has Agbo-Kpanzo thrown into prison and tortured. In vain, his daughter begs him to release Agbo-Kpanzo. Podogan turns a deaf ear. He wants the magic spell, the magic spell that will win the King's favor, the magic spell that will make him Chief Councilor and more. Never mind what this "more" is; you'll find out soon enough. Oh! I've said too much. I'd better get out of here. In the words of His Lordship, Podogan, it's a matter of life and death!

(He exits beating his drum, followed by the noisy CROWD.)

SCENE XI

(The King's Court. Enter PODOGAN, *out of breath and sweating.)*

PODOGAN: It's a matter of life and death, Your Majesty!

KING: Before you say anything, let me speak. How could you imprison and torture your own son-in-law for a story I can't make heads or tail of?

PODOGAN: Your Majesty, I tell you it's a matter of life and death.

KING: Of whose life and death? And how come?

PODOGAN: Your Majesty, I've served you faithfully for thirty years . . .

KING: Cut it short.

PODOGAN: So, anything that has to do with you is a matter of life and death.

KING: Then it has something to do with me.

PODOGAN: Yes, Your Majesty, the tortoise story.

KING: In a word, is it true or false?

PODOGAN: Your Majesty . . .

KING: Stop repeating "Your Majesty, Your Majesty." One word will suffice. The tortoise story, true or false?

PODOGAN: Your Ma . . . Forgive me. True.

KING: What?

PODOGAN: True.

KING: What is all this? Someone's idea of a joke? Or treason?

PODOGAN (*stammering*): It's . . . It's . . . It's . . .

KING (*with great severity*): Treason or a joke?

PODOGAN: Treason

KING: On whose part?

PODOGAN: Agbo-Kpanzo and his gang of crooks. They have magic power, which they use to change themselves into tortoises and sing while they're doing it.

KING: What's their game?

PODOGAN: To sow confusion in the village and then to assassinate you.

KING: Have you heard the tortoise sing? Answer yes or no.

PODOGAN: Yes.

KING: What did you hear? Be specific.

PODOGAN: Slanders, insults, threats against the local authorities.

KING: Are you lying to me, Podogan?

PODOGAN: Your Majesty, during the thirty years I've served you . . .

KING: Enough of that! Answer yes or no.

PODOGAN: No, Your Majesty.

KING: Very well, bring me Agbo-Kpanzo and the tortoise. If I catch anyone in even one little lie, I'll show the liar no mercy.

PODOGAN: For thirty years . . .

KING: Go, and go while the going is good! And bring me Agbo-Kpanzo and the tortoise!

Scene XII

(*A public square. The* KING, *the* PRIVY COUNCIL, *the* FOOL, AGBO-KPANZO, PODOGAN, *the* TORTOISE *and the* CROWD *form a circle.*)

KING (*dispensing with protocol*): A tortoise that sings? It sounds completely foolish. Nevertheless, nothing else has ever caused such commotion in our peaceful little village or stirred up my people to such a pitch. But, after mulling it all over, my intuition points out that, to the best of my knowledge, there's only one person in this village equipped to make sense of something foolish. Our Fool, himself. (*laughter and applause from the* CROWD)

FOOL: Silence, please. Every dog has his day, by which I mean we all fit in somewhere. Your Lordship, Podogan, The-King's-Most-Trusted-Councilor, answer yes or no to my questions. Is Agbo-Kpanzo your son-in-law?

PODOGAN: Yes.

FOOL: Does he have a tortoise that sings?

PODOGAN (*hesitating*): It's . . . It's . . .

FOOL: It's which? Yes or no? (PODOGAN's *embarrassment shows on his face. Mutters, even shouts, from the* CROWD.) The King will read meaning into the faces you're making. Once more, I direct you to answer yes or no. Does your son-in-law, Agbo-Kpanzo, have a tortoise that sings?

PODOGAN (*sulkily*): Yes.

FOOL: And have you heard this tortoise sing?

PODOGAN: Yes.

FOOL: And you, yourself, Your Lordship, do you have a tortoise that sings?

PODOGAN: Huh?

FOOL: Yes or no, if you don't mind. Podogan, do you have a tortoise that sings?

PODOGAN (*embarrassed*): Er . . . no.

FOOL: Do you have you a tortoise that's been singing for more than thirty years?

PODOGAN: I said, "no," and I'll stick to it.

(*Reactions from the* CROWD.)

FOOL: Silence! Now it's Agbo-Kpanzo's turn. Agbo, would you like to be the King's Chief Councilor?

AGBO: Yes.

FOOL: Do you have a tortoise that sings?

AGBO: Yes.

FOOL: Do you know a magic spell that makes it sing?

AGBO: No.

FOOL: Did your father-in-law say he had a tortoise that had been singing for thirty years?

AGBO: Yes.

PODOGAN: I said a thing like that? What a liar! When you're the one who brought that accursed tortoise into the village! Why don't you state your real plans. You want not only to be Chief Councilor but also to assassinate the King. Oh, what evil times! The truth is, the truth no longer exists.

FOOL: The truth? Difficult to distinguish. That's what we have kings for. Whatever they say is necessarily the truth. Your Majesty, let the truth come from you.

KING: Well, to tell the truth, I'm not completely sure I understand this story. That's why, once again, I'm going to rely on my intuition. It seems to me there are two tortoises, Podogan's and Agbo-Kpanzo's. So, we're going to ask each of them to make his tortoise sing. Now hear this: Anyone whose tortoise doesn't sing will die on the gallows.

PODOGAN: But . . . but . . . I . . . I . . .

KING: Hear this too: What I have said, I have said. We're going to start with Podogan's tortoise. I'll give it to the count of ten.

PODOGAN: No, Your Majesty! You can't do this. I've served you faithfully for thirty years. My only concern has been to be of some use to you. To that end, I've regularly sacrificed friends and relations. As I've seen it, it's been a matter of life and death.

KING: Excellent. And, now that you're finished, Podogan, I'll begin counting.

PODOGAN: Your Majesty!

KING: I've said what I've said, Podogan. Are you finished?

PODOGAN: Yes, I'm finished. (*He weeps.*) I'm finished. Thirty years of service.

KING: One!

PODOGAN: Thirty years of obedience.

KING: Two!

PODOGAN: Thirty years of zeal.

KING: Three!

PODOGAN: Thirty years of risk!

KING: Four!

PODOGAN: All that . . .

KING: Five!

PODOGAN: In one day . . .

KING: Six!

PODOGAN: For a measly . . .

KING: Seven!

PODOGAN: Tortoise . . .

KING: Eight!

PODOGAN: Stupidly . . .

KING: Nine!

PODOGAN: Lost!

KING: Ten! Hang him!

PODOGAN (*hysterically*): No, no, Your Majesty! I'll tell the truth. I know how much you love the truth! The tortoise, it really is Agbo-Kpanzo's; he brought it back from the forest. But I'm the one who paid people to spread the false rumor that Agbo-Kpanzo and a band of bandits were conspiring to assassinate the King. I was out to do Agbo-Kpanzo harm for competing with me to be Chief Councilor. I'm telling the truth, Your Majesty!

KING: What does our Fool think of this confession?

FOOL (*to the* CROWD): Has he told the truth? (*confused reactions from the* CROWD)

PODOGAN: I also slipped money to some people who, one morning, are to shout, "Long live King Podogan the First!"

FOOL: And now everyone can judge the true significance of your thirty years of service, loyalty, zeal, etc.

KING: Throw him into prison. And now, Agbo-Kpanzo, it's your turn.

TORTOISE (*singing*): Trouble never troubles Man.
                    It's Man who troubles Trouble.

KING: The Tortoise? The Tortoise that sings? What does the Fool have to say?

FOOL: What is there to say? (*to the* CROWD) Did Agbo-Kpanzo's Tortoise sing? Answer yes or no.

CROWD (*unanimously*): Yes! Yes!

FOOL: Well, allow me to say "No!" There's never been a tortoise that's sung since man and beast have been populating the Earth. It was all a dream. We've been carried away by Agbo-Kpanzo's dream. That's what's really happened. Agbo-Kpanzo wished to become the King's Chief Councilor not only because of the position, itself, but also because he wished to be a bigger man than his father-in-law, whom he hated. Since the honor was to go to the man the people most loved,

Agbo promised the whole village enough meat to last for a month. He went out hunting. For three days and three nights, he found nothing. For a proud and vain man like him, to have come back empty-handed would have meant humiliation. So he decided to stay in the forest until he had found and killed an animal that could fulfill his promise. Finally, exhaustion, hunger, and lack of sleep wore him down. He closed his eyes. He dreamed he was taking on animal spirits and demons his father-in-law had called up. A tortoise appeared and threatened him with its song, "Trouble never troubles Man. It's Man who troubles Trouble." It was Agbo-Kpanzo's own inner voice that was speaking to him. The hidden meaning of the tortoise's song was "Agbo, you'll come to grief not caring how you become a bigger man than your father-in-law." But Agbo preferred not to listen to this song. He woke up to discover a tortoise like any other of thousands of tortoises. He convinced himself it was the one that had sung in his dream. He caught it and brought it back to the village. You know the rest of the story. Have I spoken the truth?

CROWD (*with differing reactions*): Yes! No! It's possible! But it sang!

FOOL: Your Majesty, let the truth come from you.

KING: Agbo, do you still wish to be my Chief Councilor?

AGBO: Let the truth come from the tortoise.

KING: What does the tortoise say?

The Singing Tortoise

TORTOISE (*singing*): Trouble never troubles Man . . .

KING: What does that mean?

AGBO: That means no.

KING: And you, our Fool, you've broken the village record for popularity. You've earned the position of Chief Councilor. So what do you think?

FOOL (*after a pause*): I'll have to ask my tortoise.

KING: I see. Do you have a tortoise, too?

FOOL: Everyone has his tortoise, Your Majesty. The only difference is the bad guys no longer hear their tortoises' songs.

KING: Thus spake . . .

FOOL: The Fool.

KING: No, thus spake the King. (*with solemnity*) We, the King, through the will of all the tortoises of this village, decree the following: From this day forward, every citizen must listen to his tortoise's song. Anyone whose tortoise doesn't sing, I'll hang.

FOOL: The King has spoken. But the Fool is, come what may, the only person endowed with the privilege of speaking after the King: "Ladies and gentlemen, you are about to view as an appropriately beautiful ending for this evening's entertainment, the most magnificent, most splendiferous ballet of the Secret Society of Tortoise Men.

(DANCERS *enter costumed as tortoises. Music and ballet.*)

Jean-Luc Raharimanana was born in Antananarivo, Madagascar, in 1967. The son of a professor at the University of Madagascar, he was drawn to reading and writing early on. *The Prophet and the President* was written in 1989 and was scheduled for production at the Alliance Française of Antananarivo in 1990. Performances were postponed from month to month because of its "subversive" content. It has yet to be produced, though it received second prize in Radio France Internationale's 1990 Inter-African Theater Competition. Between the ages of 17 and 20, Raharimanana wrote poetry, filling almost 25 notebooks, and five short stories. In 1987, his poem, *Ces Mots* won second prize in a nationwide competition. In 1988, after completing a collection of poetry, *Poèmes Crematoires*, Raharimanana devoted himself to writing short stories. His story, *Lepreux*, won first prize in an international competition of French-language short stories in 1989. Raharimanana now lives in Paris where he is writing a second play and working on a collection of short stories. He is also finishing a master's thesis in ethnolinguistics at the Sorbonne.

For Ubu Repertory Theater Publications, **Stephen J. Vogel** has previously translated *Intelligence Powder* by Kateb Yacine (Algeria), *The Daughter of the Gods* by Abdou Anta Kâ (Senegal), included in the first *Afrique* anthology and *Passengers*, by Daniel Besnehard (France). His translation of Besnehard's *The White Bear* will be produced by Ubu Repertory Theater in 1992. His translation of Besnehard's *Arromanches (A Simple Death)* was given a staged reading at Ubu Repertory Theater 1990. He is co-translator of Raymond Queneau's *En Passant* presented at the French Institute/Alliance Française as part of Théâtre de la Cabriole's *Be-Bop at Saint-Germain-des-Prés*.

The premiere of the English translation of *The Prophet and The President* was directed in a staged reading by Eugene Nesmith at Ubu Repertory Theater on May 3, 1991.

CHARACTERS
(in order of appearance)

THE PROPHET
RAPIERA (*the first guard*)
RAPAOLY (*the second guard*)
THE PRESIDENT
THE MADWOMAN
and
LUNATICS (*non-speaking roles*)

(Total darkness. The voice of THE PROPHET *is heard.)*

THE PROPHET:

Yes, I blaspheme . . .
My God, the little that I am
against the all that thou art.
Give me a mountain
against a bit of sand
O capitalist spirit
To hope for all against so little.
My God, I am a worm
a worm that will gnaw at your guts.
My God, your bounty knows no limits:
Someone kicks you in the ass
and you keep smiling,
someone nails you to a pole
and you save us from evil!
My God, what masochism!

(pause)

Bible! Terror!
Apocalypse, end of the world.
You infidels! The dragons of hell
will chew you up forever!
It is said that my tongue will be flame,
my skin flame, my fingers serpents.
But my thing, they don't mention that.
My eyes, yes, my eyes: chasms.
The devil is flame, hell is flame,
The Holy Ghost is also flame.
Little flame that walks over our heads
driving us mad, mad,

read the bible, you'll have eternity!
And I, I who care
only for my own life,
I, who see nothing beyond
my own existence, which is a real bitch . . .
Mightn't there be more of a short-term hope?
Yes! Yes!
Pray, follow the Way of the Cross.

FIRST PICTURE

FIRST PANEL

(*Lights up on a madhouse cell. Two cots side by side in a corner of the stage. Stage right, a closed door.* LUNATICS *present, but not speaking or moving.*)

THE PROPHET (*striding across the apron of the stage*): It's obvious, I'm nuts. It's nice to be nuts, you can say anything. Who, me? I was out of my head! I'm blocking the road? Oh, the road doesn't mind! What the road wants is a little asphalt. Some hard asphalt, some nice black tar.

Me, blaspheme? Heck! The inquisition . . . But all that is over with. Freedom of speech! I won't even be excommunicated by our dear Pope. I was possessed by a devil. A little exorcism will do the trick.

Oh my God, forgive me all my sins . . . since I'm going to start in again tomorrow . . . (*He runs to the door.*) Open the door! Open it or I'll smash everything!

RAPIERA (*offstage*): He's really getting on my nerves!

THE PROPHET (*banging on the door*): Open it! Open it!

RAPAOLY (*offstage*): Shut yer trap!

THE PROPHET: My trap? Whaddya mean, my trap? (*He starts humming.*) What's wrong with my trap? I . . . I . . . (*He abruptly changes his tone.*) Yes! I am a saint. A modern-day saint. I'll escape from here, I will! Fly away . . . I'll go looking for the gods! Me, I'll take a plane. I'll take the Challenger and dash up to heaven . . . I'd land in paradise, I'd make a paradisiac landing in the midst of the dumbfounded angels, angels running every which way.

(*He gestures broadly.*)

Greetings, Good Lord! I come from the earth. No! I'm not a Martian. Nor the Devil, either . . . I am the Prophet: I've come to work out a mutual accord.

Let's shake hands! Not hard! I've got a pretty good grip myself! There's flesh, and muscles! Oh, you've already got an accord like that? Shit! You don't want to accept my contract? I want to keep my body in paradise. I want to enjoy my body! No? You mean you've got to lose your body to get a lifetime of paradise, the most beautiful life of all lives? Paradise, paradise, paradise, dice, dice . . .

SECOND PANEL

(RAPIERA *and* RAPAOLY *enter abruptly.*)

RAPIERA: You get a good grip on him. This will calm him down. (*He holds up a syringe.* THE PROPHET *backs up to the far end of the stage.*)

THE PROPHET: Back, you fiend! (*to himself*) Paradise, a life without vices, misfortunes, shrieks and sufferings! Oh my masochism, you're really going to tie one on! No more for you the pleasure of suffering!

(RAPIERA *and* RAPAOLY *grab him. He pretends to give in, then he frees himself, abruptly.*)

And you, you pretty scoundrel, you'll get your ass burned! Sitting down! You'll be sitting down . . . No more outbursts, tumbling or acrobatics.

(RAPAOLY *edges toward him, carefully.*)

Get back! Greedy lips, firm breasts, slithering hips, furtive flesh, burning crotch, love-sweat, all phffft! Out the window!

(RAPIERA *and* RAPAOLY *pin him down at last, giving him an injection.*)

We won't be men anymore in paradise!

(*As the injection begins to take effect, he drops quietly into the arms of* RAPAOLY.)

RAPIERA: What a loony.

RAPAOLY: This bastard is heavy . . . (*He stretches him out on the floor.*) Look at him now. He looks like a baby.

RAPIERA: Come on! You sound like you're sorry for him.

RAPAOLY: No, but sometimes I envy him . . . He's got the guts to say what's on his mind.

RAPIERA: Well, all it takes is to be crazy, or else to just love pris . . . I mean rest homes.

RAPAOLY: But him, all he sees and talks about is paradise.

RAPIERA: Yeah, right, as soon as he gets out of hell . . .

RAPAOLY: Or the tunnel . . . (*There is a sudden shout offstage.*) There's Number Eight, throwing one of his fits. (*They exit quickly. A long pause. Only* THE PROPHET *can be seen, stretched out on the stage. Other shouts are heard, then footsteps.*)

RAPIERA (*offstage*): Hold him tight, for God's sake!

(*More footsteps.* RAPIERA *and* RAPAOLY *re-enter with another lunatic,* THE PRESIDENT. *He looks haggard and indignant.*)

RAPAOLY: The other ones always beat up on this guy.

RAPIERA: Whoever heard of calling yourself a president! Totally nuts!

RAPAOLY: We haven't tried him with the Prophet yet.

RAPIERA: Let's hope they get along.

RAPAOLY: A president and a prophet . . . that's usually good for a few sparks.

RAPIERA: No, a king and a prophet is what you mean.

RAPAOLY: Six of one, half a dozen of the other . . . Ha ha, heavenly power and earthly power. "Foreigners seem to fight among themselves . . ." [1] (*They exit.*)

THIRD PANEL

(THE PRESIDENT *looks around. A red ribbon crosses his upper torso, like a sash. He notices a stick lying on the floor and picks it up. With his hands behind his back, he begins to inspect the area all around him. Condescending gestures to everyone. Finally, he sees* THE PROPHET.)

THE PRESIDENT: No sleeping while on duty, citizen!

(*He shakes him by one foot, the other does not move.* THE PRESIDENT *looks around, making sure that the other* LU-NATICS *see him, then he puts one foot on the outstretched body. Hands on hips, he changes his position several times, as if being photographed. Raising his hand with the stick , he shouts.*)

Long live the Republic of My Deals!

(*He drops his pose and starts to pace back and forth.*)

What a shame that the Republic won't accept a king! But as for me, I shall become president for life, to make up for it. If they won't bow down to me, at least I'll have the satisfaction of seeing all those people lick my boots.

At first I was truthful, I really was, but they wouldn't listen to me. Now you're all against me.

I can take care of myself, Sir, Madam, Miss. It is my pleasure to inform you that it was they who led the country to the abyss. I'd like to arrest those traitors.

I'd like to see them hanged.

(*The other* LUNATICS *stand up silently, threateningly.*)

61

Threats? So I'm a tyrant? All right, I give up . . .
But history will show you your stupidity! (*aside*) They
had me there, I gave in . . . But I'm trickier than
they are. I'm going to neutralize them, one at a time.
Pow! Pow!

(*He makes a face. Seeing the body of* THE PROPHET *still on
the floor, he again goes through the same poses as before,
changing position. He puts the stick in his mouth, imitating
the movements of someone enjoying a long cigar. Meanwhile,
the body under his foot begins to move.* THE PRESIDENT
goes to inspect the stage again.)

Is the thermostat working well? (*pause*) Good, good.
We'll have to put a little grease on all this. (*pause*) Yes?
Yes, who? (*pause*) That's right! Speak up! Yes, Mr.
President. Yes, Mr. President.

(THE PROPHET *wakes up, feels his head, and gets up with
some difficulty. He takes a few unsteady steps. Upon seeing*
THE PRESIDENT, *he cries out.*)

THE PROPHET: My people! Here are my people!

THE PRESIDENT (*turning toward him*): Ah my adviser,
Here's my adviser.

THE PROPHET: People, hear me . . .

THE PRESIDENT: That's right, let's hear your report.

THE PROPHET: Man has broken God's heart. Man has
cut off the Devil's tail. Can it be that Man is the
stronger?

The Prophet and The President

THE PRESIDENT: Now that's a truly pertinent question. Truly pertinent.

THE PROPHET: God and the Devil are fighting to seduce Man. Can it be that Man is the more attractive?

THE PRESIDENT: Yes indeed, your remark is well founded. Necessary measures must be taken.

THE PROPHET: God cannot live in hell. The Devil cannot live in heaven. Man lives a life partly hellish, partly heavenly. Can it be that Man is the more adaptable?

THE PRESIDENT: Well! If that's how it is, cordon off the university so that the students cannot take to the streets. Say that the Jirama is doing some construction work. Send the buses back to the garages. Inform the Minister of the Interior. Put guards outside the radio station. And let us know when it's all over, otherwise impose a curfew.

THE PROPHET: God is unhappy, the Devil still more so. But Man has a good time; he laughs, he jokes around despite the shadow of death. Can it be that death is the supreme condition?

THE PRESIDENT: Of course, I've already said so. Go on! Now for the execution . . . (*He loses interest in everything.*)

THE PROPHET: People! God is not dead. He wants to die. In order to die, God wants to become Man. He already tried it once, but it was a failure. Christ came back to life. It was a failure, a failure.

(The President *goes up to a wall of the cell, where his shadow can be seen. He fixes his ribbon a bit, and dusts it off. He contemplates his shadow.*)

The Prophet: People, God is coming back in force, this time. The hour is at hand. The signs have already appeared: earthquake, pollution, war, cyclone, cataclysm, disaster in the air, dictator, racism. Everything is caving in on our heads so that Heaven will look to us like the promised land.

(*aside*) Like any jerks, they'd go rushing into heaven, and God would take advantage of the situation to take our place on earth . . . Finally, He'll have a good time. And He'll be afraid of dying. And as for us men, we'll be miserable in heaven, sad as a God.

(*After a pause,* The Prophet *assumes the pose of a visionary, preaching a sermon.*)

In heaven all take their rest beside the vine. Peace, there will be peace!

The President: Peace . . . (*He remains facing his shadow.*) Peace . . . Do like me, if you want peace . . . Promise them everything and blame all mistakes on other people.

The Prophet (*addressing the* Lunatics): Peace will damn you to inactivity.

The President: Do nothing, let rumor do its job. The people will follow you.

The Prophet: But I, as prophet, I am God. I can do

64

everything. I have no need of heaven. (*He takes some pebbles from his pocket, spits on them, then places them about the stage.*) Saint, saint, art thou Radada, red cock, night bird's child . . . I give, I give not, monster half-human half-animal . . . [2] (*He kisses the ground several times.*)

THE PRESIDENT (*seeing this*): You see? He bows down willingly before me. I had no need to make the slightest sign nor give a single order.

THE PROPHET (*getting up, abruptly*): Sacrilege, accursed one! (*He strikes* THE PRESIDENT.)

THE PRESIDENT: Help, treason, help! Save your beloved president . . . (RAPIERA *and* RAPAOLY *enter and subdue* THE PROPHET.)

THE PRESIDENT: Good, good! Very good, my brave fellow citizens. Tomorrow, I'll appoint you both ministers.

THE PROPHET (*trying to break free*): Cursed be those who would keep Man in his ignorance. Man is a God. (*speaking directly to the* LUNATICS) A God, a God!

THE PRESIDENT: Lord! What an ungrateful populace! I give them housing and jobs and this is what I get in return . . .

THE PROPHET: Thou, thou art merely an unclean beast.

THE PRESIDENT: Insults . . .

65

THE PROPHET: Thou shalt rot from thy entrails.

THE PRESIDENT: Curses . . .

THE PROPHET (*pushed towards the exit by* RAPIERA *and* RAPAOLY): Man, whom God envies, thou shalt never know.

THE PRESIDENT: Misunderstanding . . . (THE PROPHET, RAPIERA *and* RAPAOLY *exit.*) slander and gossip. (*The screams of* THE PROPHET *can be heard.*) The Age of Kings! Oh, the good old days! Now, anybody can seize power. There's no more absolute power. I want a power which is absolute, absolute, absolute . . . absolution!

(He goes toward one of the cots, sits down on it as if he were sitting on a throne. He appears to be lost in deep thought.)

FOURTH PANEL

(RAPIERA *and* RAPAOLY *re-enter, dragging the inert body of* THE PROPHET *by the shoulders.*)

RAPAOLY: You're sure that . . .

RAPIERA: Sure, there's no risk involved. Give me a hand.

(*They stretch the body out on the other bed.* THE PRESIDENT *holds the same pose as before.*)

RAPAOLY: What's wrong with that one?

RAPIERA: You tell me!

RAPAOLY: Really nuts. (*He looks at* THE PROPHET.) But still, you dope him and you're playing with fire.

RAPIERA: Nah, he'll take it with no problem. He'll sleep for a half a day and then everything will get back to normal.

RAPAOLY: His eyes are still wide open . . . (RAPIERA *shrugs his shoulders and exits.*) Hey! (RAPAOLY *tries to waken* THE PROPHET *from his stupor.*) Hey! (*Finally,* RAPAOLY *gives up trying and starts to exit but then changes his mind and returns.*)

THE PRESIDENT (*abruptly ceasing his meditation*): Oh, adviser! My good man, I think I've found the solution.

RAPAOLY: Shit, now this one'll bug me!

67

THE PRESIDENT: Yes, it is I, the one they slander, who have nonetheless solved the problem.

RAPAOLY: Take it easy, mustn't get him excited.

THE PRESIDENT: Here's what we'll do. Firstly, a coup d'état. Secondly, set up a dictatorship, that way the power will become absolute once again and more useful for the development of the country. Thirdly . . .

RAPAOLY: Thirdly, Mr. President-for-Life?

THE PRESIDENT: Thirdly, thirdly . . .

RAPAOLY: Thirdly, you, Mr. President, are going to sit quietly in your corner and not bother people with your big mouth.

THE PRESIDENT: Thirdly . . . Come now, as my minister did you not pay particular attention to the political strategy which I outlined to you yesterday?

RAPAOLY: You know you're really starting to sound like one of those crackpot Third World presidents?

THE PRESIDENT: Oh? Well, please be good enough to read me what you wrote down.

RAPAOLY: What I wrote down? But . . . oh, I forgot that you're nuts. Just as nuts as those presidents who build huge palaces with atom bomb shelters and everything. They should all be killed off, those presidents, the bastards. They're worse than Hitler and the Devil put together. Hitler, at least you can say he tried to make his country the master of the world, but you . . . you're just trying to make us the masters of the have-nots. We can't even fool ourselves into thinking there's a struggle going on. Just have-nots for days.

THE PRESIDENT: Good! Thirdly, you'll address me as Mr. Dictator General.

RAPAOLY: Shit, Mr. Dictator.

THE PRESIDENT: I said, "Mr. Dictator General."

RAPAOLY: Shit, Mr. Dictator General.

THE PRESIDENT: Good, you must always say "Mr. Dictator General." But mind it doesn't get around. Only those closest to me may address me thus, otherwise there'd be another scandal.

RAPAOLY: Now, you're going to shut up. (*He forces* THE PRESIDENT *to sit down on the bed.*)

THE PRESIDENT: As minister you disappoint me greatly. You're relieved of your duties.

RAPAOLY: That's right, that's right, handsome.

THE PRESIDENT: You're no longer the Minister of the Armed Forces, you'll go to prison, into exile . . . to the Ministry of Culture.

(*While this is going on* THE PROPHET *tosses about on his bed, moaning.*)

RAPAOLY (*letting go of* THE PRESIDENT): Hey! It looks as though the Prophet is out for the count. Hey! Yo!

(*He shakes* THE PROPHET *while* THE PRESIDENT *takes advantage of this to exit quickly.*)

Rapiera! Come here quick! Hell! Now the President's escaped. Rapiera!

(*He runs to get his partner, exiting the stage.* THE PROPHET *tosses about still more. He is experiencing spasmodic seizures. He gets up, like a sleep-walker, his gaze distant, his arms stretched upwards. He staggers forward.*)

THE PROPHET: Thou, O God. Thou . . . suicide, suicide is a power thou canst not have. Man alone can bring about his own death. A God cannot put an end to his own existence.

Thou, O God, art condemned to be, to be eternally, with the responsibility for thine own soul, thine own essence, with the weight of thine own perfection. The earth . . . thou hast created it, but canst thou live on it? Canst thou?

(*He falls to his knees, curling up in a fetal position while* RAPIERA *and* RAPAOLY *enter, hurriedly.*)

RAPIERA: No, I tell you. I haven't seen the President.

THE PROPHET: God in chains . . . slave of Love. Sad God.

RAPAOLY: He's raving.

RAPIERA: Come on, we'll take him to the infirmary. (RAPIERA and RAPAOLY *carry him off. Slow fade.*)

SECOND PICTURE

FIRST PANEL

(*In the medical storeroom. There are crates and boxes spread out all around.* THE PRESIDENT *stands in front of a skeleton which lacks an arm. The skeleton is hung from above by a string. Its feet dangle a few centimeters above the floor. The exit leads to an unseen stairway.*)

THE PRESIDENT: Hmmm! I need a shave. (*He studies the skeleton as if it were his reflection in a mirror.*) Beards are out of style. Castro is castrated. (*He plucks an imaginary hair from his smooth chin.*) Set up a dictatorship, yes, but with a new look. A liberal dictatorship! Political freedom, freedom of speech. I let people speak, then I dictate to them. Obey your president's decrees! (*pause*) Huh, gotta get a shave. Oh, what's this? (*There is a small spot on the skeleton's forehead. He touches his own forehead.*) Why, it's nothing but a little dust. It seems to me I've spent more than enough time greeting this UN representative. The rights of Man? Oh, sir . . . Well, I've got to run now, a speech to give to my cabinet.

(RAPAOLY *and* RAPIERA'S *voices are heard offstage.*)

RAPAOLY: He's bound to be downstairs, in the storeroom.

RAPIERA: That's the only place we haven't looked.

RAPAOLY: A president on the lam, that's pretty funny, isn't it . . .

72

RAPIERA (*laughingly*): Now where's he gone to, this president?

RAPAOLY (*in the same vein*): He's down in the cellar of his palace. (*Their steps are heard on the stairs.*) And the prophet? Did you tie him up good?

RAPIERA: He'd need a miracle . . .

THE PRESIDENT: Ah, here come my ministers.

(RAPAOLY *and* RAPIERA *enter.*)

THE PRESIDENT: My chief advisers! Come in. Today our nation turns a new page in its history. (*The two guards make a move to surround him.*) How about a scotch first? (*He makes an about-face and goes to a crate, from which he removes two bottles of medicine.*)

RAPIERA: Shit, he's not going to drink those! There's nothing here but old medicine.

RAPAOLY: Here, let me. (*speaking to* THE PRESIDENT) It's a great honor, Mr. President . . .

THE PRESIDENT: Mr.?

RAPAOLY: Mr. Dictator General.

THE PRESIDENT: Who? Mr. Dictator what?

RAPAOLY: But it would be even better if we could enjoy it outside.

THE PRESIDENT: Quite right! Let's go . . . (*He gives the bottles to the guards.*) Bring some glasses, too. Ah, it's nice to have ministers that are jacks-of-all-trades. They even wait on tables.

(RAPAOLY *starts forward and is the first to exit followed by* THE PRESIDENT.)

Rapiera: Mr. Dictator General! (*He laughs.*) No, at this rate he's going to be emperor. No, better yet, a new incarnation of God.

(*He starts through the doorway when suddenly the sound of a struggle is heard, coming from the stairway.* RAPAOLY *and* THE PRESIDENT *tumble back in, whereupon* THE PROPHET *enters in a violent rage.*)

THE PROPHET: It was you, you who tied me up. But nothing can hold me back. Today is the Day of Destruction.

RAPAOLY (*moaning on the floor*): My knee, my knee . . .

(THE PRESIDENT *stands up with difficulty.*)

RAPIERA: Hey, this guy's getting dangerous. (*He takes a step forward.*)

THE PROPHET: Don't move.

(THE PRESIDENT *goes towards the the skeleton.*)

THE PROPHET (*pointing to* THE PRESIDENT): You, too.

(THE PRESIDENT *isn't even listening and continues walking toward his objective.* THE PROPHET *leaps at his throat.* RAPIERA *seizes the chance to try and overcome* THE PROPHET. *A struggle ensues.* THE PRESIDENT *frees himself, nimbly. The momentum of their struggle hurls* THE PROPHET *and* RAPIERA *through the doorway. They fight on the stairway.* RAPAOLY *tries to get up, but in vain. Then a cry is heard, and* THE PROPHET *re-enters, without* RAPIERA. THE PRESIDENT *rubs the nape of his neck in front of the skeleton.*)

THE PROPHET: Day of Destruction! People, heaven is promised you, but first you must go through hell. You must endure the end of the world, and observe the destruction of your universe. Has this God no shame?

Why does He crush me with His might? Day of Destruction! Why wait for a God to do it, this destruction?

(THE PROPHET *goes after* RAPAOLY, *kicking him in the stomach, crushing his knees.* THE PRESIDENT *turns around and contemplates the scene with a calm and steady gaze.* RAPAOLY *avoids these blows by rolling about the floor. While doing so, he loses his keys. A final kick makes him pass out. Turning away from him,* THE PROPHET *rushes to the crates, and tips them over. Bottles roll across the floor.*)

THE PROPHET: Ah! The triumph of a God: total destruction, pervasive evil. On the day the world ends, on the day of the Apocalypse, God bursts with glory. No more Man, no more. God takes over Evil.

(*He heaves a box far away.* THE PRESIDENT *continues to watch with a steady gaze. Finally,* THE PROPHET *spots the keys. He picks them up, and dashes to the exit. He is then heard in the stairway.* THE PRESIDENT *trots over to the door to glance outside, slyly.*)

THE PROPHET (*offstage*): Mercenaries of the earth, come out! (*He is answered by the screams of madmen. At once what sounds like a pack of wild animals is heard. The* LUNATICS *from the other cells have been set free.*) Come out and destroy what you have built, before a God destroys it!

THE PRESIDENT: An uprising of the masses! (*The screams of the "masses" grow louder.*) They want to kill me! I don't want to die! NO!

THE PROPHET: (*offstage*): You are the sons of Man. You rule over everything living on Earth. Destroy everything! EVERYTHING! Display your might, your power to destroy. Let no stone remain standing.

(*From offstage grinding and snapping noises, and numerous other sounds, can be heard.*)

Why should anyone want to restrict Man to the Earth? Ha! It's God who is restricted. All He can do is good, despite all His rages and His might.

THE PRESIDENT (*speaking to the offstage voice*): Hey! You doing all the shouting! I've known thousands of rabble-rousers in my time, but I'm still on my throne. You hold the crowds while they're elated, but I hold onto them by the stomach, by the guts.

(*A piercing scream suddenly rises above the others.* RAPAOLY, *still unconscious, starts abruptly then stirs about.*)

THE PROPHET (*offstage*): Man, yes, Man can do both good and evil at the same time. Not God, not the Devil. God is only Good, the Devil is only Evil.

(RAPAOLY *regains consciousness.*)

Man is the product of God and the Devil. Man is the true sin of God, His delirium, His madness, His hallucination . . . Man, Man, Man, ah! MAN!

(*His cry is lost in the screams of the other* LUNATICS. RAPAOLY *gets to his feet with much difficulty and limps over to the door. He takes a quick look outside and then shuts the door hastily. He leans against it, looking terrified.*)

77

RAPAOLY: They're all out in the hallway.

THE PRESIDENT: Oh yes, you might well say that. We are all out in the hallway.

RAPAOLY: They're all out in the hallway.

THE PRESIDENT: But I'd rather be in the hallway than in the tunnel!

RAPAOLY: They're playing with Rapiera's body.

THE PRESIDENT: Oh you know, in the dark . . .

RAPAOLY: They're dragging him by his feet, his eyeballs are hanging down on his cheeks.

THE PRESIDENT: No one will notice.

RAPAOLY: They're dragging him by his feet, his arms are all twisted, his tongue is coming out of his mouth.

THE PRESIDENT: It's clear that you're not accustomed to holding power! (*pause*) All right! To cheer you up, I'm going to name you . . . let's see, let's see . . . Minister of Justice? How's that? And now let's get busy with the counterrevolution . . .

RAPAOLY: They got him. They got him. Afterwards, it'll be my turn, it'll be my turn, my turn . . .

(RAPAOLY's *back slowly slides down the door, and he ends up sitting on the floor, sobbing.*)

THE PRESIDENT: Oh, don't take it so seriously! The people are never satisfied. They've always got to have something to grumble about. That's no reason to get all teary-eyed. Come on! Buck up.

RAPAOLY: Buck up, he says. For once, you're right, you poor loony.

(*The screams subside and grow more distant.*)

THIRD PANEL

THE PRESIDENT: Things seem to have quieted down.

RAPAOLY: How the hell did I get into this mess? The doctor said, "There are fifty loonies and three boxes of tranquilizers. Work it out for yourselves. We'll come by once a week." Even knowing all that, I still said yes.

THE PRESIDENT: Things have quieted down, Minister.

RAPAOLY: Oh, sure. Things have quieted down, things have quieted down. People always say that, "Things have quieted down." But what about tomorrow?

THE PRESIDENT: Rest assured, Minister, tomorrow I shall still be president. The economy is making strides, look at the statistics. Our foreign debts are paid off, and never before has the literacy rate been this high. There's no reason on earth why I should step down now, when the country's affairs are going so well.

RAPAOLY: For a country whose affairs are going well, this country's affairs are going real well, real wellwellwell . . .

THE PRESIDENT: Before this, did we ever have any billionaires among us? No. Now there are dozens and dozens. Our citizens are growing ever richer. (*He addresses the offstage* LUNATICS.) Didn't I just give you a raise? Only a real hypocrite would say the country is going downhill. And who is it leading the country forward? Me!

80

The Prophet and The President

(*The inmates are heard, as if running in a pack. There is a knocking on the door.* THE PRESIDENT *is panic-stricken.*)

They're coming back! We must have a counterrevolution. Quick, quick!

RAPAOLY: Fifty, there are fifty of them!

(*He gets up, hobbles over to the skeleton, and takes it down. Then he stands by the door.*)

Come in, come right in, Mr. Loony and Company. You'll find the right person to talk to.

(*The door opens noisily. We see* THE PROPHET *and some of the LUNATICS in silhouette.* RAPAOLY *dances bizarrely with the skeleton.*)

THE PROPHET: Stand back, stand back, we are in the kingdom of Death, in the sacred kingdom.

THE PRESIDENT: Saved!

(RAPAOLY *collapses. The door remains open.*)

RAPAOLY: I can't take it, my leg, it's hurting me, I'm hurting.

THE PROPHET (*offstage*): The kingdom of Death, that's where we mortals will end up. Death is our true God.

THE PRESIDENT (*to* RAPAOLY): What a splendid idea, my dear counselor, brandishing an image of me, in order to frighten these people. Now do you believe that no one, absolutely no one, can depose me?

THE PROPHET: Death has no need of priest or preachers to make his presence felt. Death is in us. We carry it about from birth, and with each breath of life it grows, it grows.

THE PRESIDENT: Even the opposition . . . phffft! All in my hip pocket.

THE PROPHET (*still offstage*): People! The supreme power belongs to Death. Lift your voices in song and worship your God, Death.

(*Singing*) LUNATICS:

> *Your money*
> *Will not lead you to the tomb*
> *Your family*
> *Will carry you toward the tomb.*[3]

RAPAOLY: I'm going to go nuts, too! All this talk about Death, about revolution, about, about . . . (*He is at a loss for words.*) But what about me? What's going to happen to me in this thing? (*Dragging one leg, he crawls over to a crate.*)

THE PRESIDENT: I am Master of the country. (*pause*) The only thing I have to fear is the I.M.F. and the UN.

(*The* LUNATICS *take up the chorus of the song, again and again.*)

THE PROPHET AND THE PRESIDENT

THE PRESIDENT: A president does not serve the Nation, he is in the service of Money, and Money is the Nation.

THE PROPHET (*offstage*): Let us dance, O people, dance to the glory of our God.

(*The sound of trampling feet is heard. At times a foot projects through the partly-opened door.*)

THE PRESIDENT: Now those crazy agitators have started dancing. (*He stands stiffly before the door.*) Dance, dance. It'll take more than some worthless, shantytown bums like you to give me a restless night. (*He slams the door.*)

THE PROPHET (*offstage*): Hear our prayer, O Lord. Close not the door to thy kingdom on us. Turn not thy back on us. Thou art Death, which we mortals shall one day be. Thou art our Destiny, our Finality. Thou art the end of existence, which is a real bitch.

THE PRESIDENT: Who's that talking, shouting, stirring up trouble? Some student, some sociologist, some journalist? (*He looks about him and notices* RAPAOLY *trying to pry open a crate.*) Ah ha! I caught you, Minister, trying to force open the State Coffers.

RAPAOLY (*finally getting the crate open*): What the! . . . There's nothing but empty bottles in all this junk.

(*He turns the crate upside down, and the bottles roll all over the floor.*)

THE PRESIDENT: And just what do you expect to find in the State Coffers, Minister? Nothing, nothing at all . . . Go give Switzerland a try.

RAPAOLY: Drugs, I need drugs to ease the pain. (*He drags himself over to another crate.*) Nothing, nothing!

THE PRESIDENT: Of course there's nothing! (*pause*) Cyclone . . . How soon will you be back with some international relief for us? U.S. dollars, Japanese Yen, French Francs. (*He counts on his fingers and licks his chops.*)

RAPAOLY: Well, I guess he's not as nuts as I thought.

(*Meanwhile, the voice of* THE PROPHET *is heard, repeating his prayer, over and over.*)

THE PROPHET (*offstage*): Hear our prayer, O Lord . . .

THE PRESIDENT: Cyclone! Whoosh! The tide is rising, the villages are engulfed. In the rice paddies, the water is rising. Glug glug glug glug . . . drowned bodies everywhere and victims of disaster. The city is 200% destroyed. I see it from my helicopter. I'm flying over the country. I'm taking note of the damage, before I have my siesta. My siesta, that's sacred. Don't wake me unless there's a coup d'état. Whoosh! Cyclone, low pressure system . . .

(*He suddenly notices* RAPAOLY.)

What? You didn't drown? The more victims we have, the more international relief we receive.

(*He descends on* RAPAOLY *and strikes him mercilessly.*)

Die! Die!

(*A muffled noise is heard coming from the other side of the door, like a litany intoned by a crowd.*)

You must die, die in the service of the Nation.

(*He holds up a crate and then brings it crashing down on* RAPAOLY's *head.*)

There you are! Galant martyr for the Revolution.

THE PROPHET (*offstage, as the murmuring increases*): It is Death performing his divine duty.

THE PRESIDENT (*addressing* RAPAOLY's *corpse*): Citizen, you were struck down by the enemies of the Revolution. We shall find the guilty party. We shall find a guilty party. (*He shouts to the audience.*) Is there a guilty party in the house? (*The murmuring grows to the intensity of a scream.*)

THE PROPHET (*offstage*): People, your God summons you. Heed his call!

THE PRESIDENT: A guilty party, I want a guilty party! (*He grabs the skeleton.*) My Lord Justices, here is your guilty party! (*He throws the skeleton to the floor.*)

FOURTH PANEL

(THE PROPHET *and the other* LUNATICS *spill through the doorway. The skeleton lies beside* RAPAOLY.)

THE PROPHET: Assassin! Thou hast slain our God!

(*The other* LUNATICS *swarm over* THE PRESIDENT, *striking him. A brawl ensues.* THE PROPHET *takes the skeleton in his arms. A* MADWOMAN *stands off to one side. She cradles a doll in her arms.*)

THE MADWOMAN: Sleep child! Sleep child! [4] (*She turns to the other* LUNATICS.) Quiet! You'll wake up my baby.

(THE PRESIDENT *succeeds in breaking free. In his haste to escape, he runs into* THE MADWOMAN. *The doll falls to the floor.*)

THE MADWOMAN: My baby, my baby . . .

(*The other* LUNATICS *run after* THE PRESIDENT, *stepping on the doll and kicking it across the stage.*)

THE MADWOMAN: My baby! They've stolen my baby.

(THE PRESIDENT *climbs atop some crates and bares his teeth.*)

THE PRESIDENT: Get back! I'm your president. I hold all the power. One wave of my hand and your doom is sealed. Get back!

(*Again he bares his teeth. The other* LUNATICS *move back, in awe of him.*)

THE PROPHET: Who art thou that dar'st speak of doom to the people of Death?

THE PRESIDENT (*proudly, while adjusting his ribbon*): I am the Supreme Commander of the Military. I am the Lord Chief Justice. I am the one who charts the economic and financial course of the country. I am the one who directs the representatives and the National Assembly. I am the one who dictates government policy. I am the Guiding Force of the Revolution.

THE PROPHET: Thou hast slain our God. (*He shows the skeleton which he holds in his arms.*) This day shall be for thee the day of the last judgment.

THE MADWOMAN (*locating her baby*): Oh, my tiny child, he's dead. (*She holds up the doll, which now has only one leg.*) He ate my baby's leg. (*She rushes at* THE PRESIDENT.) Child-snatcher! Ogre![5] You killed my child!

(THE PRESIDENT *falls. The other* LUNATICS *descend on him while* THE PROPHET *stretches the skeleton out on a crate, improvising a kind of altar.*)

THE PROPHET: People, our God is resting eternally. But their Gods, those of the pagans, the heretics, endure eternal life, endure the hell of endless existence.

(*The other* LUNATICS *are not even listening to him. One* LUNATIC *is the first to notice a medicine bottle on the floor. He picks it up, looks down the neck, then lifts it to his lips. A second* LUNATIC *fights him for it. A third drags the body of*

87

THE PRESIDENT *by the feet, but drops it in order to open a crate on which is marked, in large red letters, the word "ACID".)*

THE PROPHET: Eternal death, no rebirth, no resurrection, the eternity of Death.

(He utters a sharp cry, like a dog. The third LUNATIC *pulls a full bottle out of the crate. He drinks it in one gulp and falls down dead. His body shakes spasmodically, then goes stiff. The second* LUNATIC *looks in the crate. He takes out a bottle. Immediately, the* LUNATICS *swarm around the crate. Each battles for a drink and, one by one, they fall down dead, all except* THE PROPHET *and* THE MADWOMAN.)

THE PROPHET: Eternal death, eternal death . . .

Fifth Panel

(The Prophet *falls to his knees among the bodies stretched out around him.*)

The Madwoman: Oh my baby. They killed my baby. (*She cradles the doll in her arms.*)

The Prophet: Woman! Do not weep for your baby! Rather, rejoice. Sing, dance. Sing and dance. Death is the ultimate Good that can befall us in this life. Dance, sing.

(The Madwoman *wanders around the stage, stepping over bodies.*)

The Madwoman: My baby is dead, my baby is dead.

The Prophet (*getting to his feet*): Sing, dance. Death is among us. (*He lifts the torso of one of the* Lunatics *stretched out on the floor.*) Not bad looking, right? (*He does the same with another body.*) Look how happy he is. (*He moves on to another body.*) And this one? (*He looks at* The Madwoman.) No? Don't you like him? (*He moves on to still another body, that of* The President.) Look!

The Madwoman: He's the one, he's the one who killed my baby.

(*She rushes to* The Prophet *who is holding* The President *and hits both of them with the doll.*)

The Prophet: Back, you bitch! Fear me. I am the guardian of the dead.

THE MADWOMAN: But he's the one who killed my baby. He's the one. Without him, my baby would still be alive. Without him, we'd be happy. (*She points to* THE PRESIDENT *each time.*) Without him, I wouldn't have suffered. Without him, my baby would have known what life really is. Without him the world would be so beautiful. And you, you, you're still defending him. (*She throws the doll in* THE PROPHET's *face.*)

THE PROPHET: Bitch! What hope do you think there is for you in loving life? You'll be subject to the power of men in life. You'll be subject to the power of the State, and tyrants, and dictators. You'll be a slave to your stomach, to your womb. Your fate will be whatever a God throws your way. You'll give birth in pain and your man will sweat his life away. You'll be subject to the unyielding standards of Society. You won't be living in life! You'll give in. (*For a moment they stand, motionless.*) Come! Come with me into the kingdom of Death. There you can truly live. Live, because there there is neither God, nor law, nor master, nor tyrant, nor need nor necessity. Come!

(*They stare at each other.* THE PROPHET *holds out his hand.* THE MADWOMAN *approaches him. She steps on the lost leg of the doll. Then she realizes what it is.*)

THE MADWOMAN (*picking up the doll's leg*): My child, where is my child?

THE PROPHET: Come! I am the prophet for whom Mankind has been waiting.

THE MADWOMAN: No! You're only the Devil. Go away, go away! (*She pushes him towards the door.*) Go away.

THE PROPHET: Come, come with me. (*He tries to drag her with him.*)

THE MADWOMAN: Let me go! (*Only* THE PROPHET's *hand can still be seen, sticking through the doorway, squeezing* THE MADWOMAN's *wrist.*) Leave me alone! (*She breaks away, violently, and closes the door. Then she rushes over to the doll and sticks the leg back on it.*) Oh, my darling baby. You're alive, aren't you? You're alive! (*She bumps into a body.*) No! Don't look. The world is full of bad men, full of suffering, but I love you, I love you. My love will protect you.

THE PROPHET (*offstage*): Woman! I'll be back someday. Someday you'll be mine. Mine! (*A dismal laugh is heard.*)

THE MADWOMAN: Sleep, my baby, sleep. Don't listen. I love you.

(*The lights slowly dim. Curtain.*)

TRANSLATOR'S NOTES

In the original production, several lines and passages were spoken in Malagasy, an Indonesian language, which along with French, is an official language of Madagascar. These passages are cited below in the original Malagasy.

1. page 60. A proverbial expression: *"Vazahas mody miady!"*

2. page 65. *"Mazimazi! Masina ianao Radada, akoholahimena, zanam-borondolo, homeko tsy homeko, la lamasinina, bibiolona sakelimihoajore . . .*

3. page 82. From a popular song in Madagascar:

    Io volabenao io ô
    Tsy hitondra anao any amin'ny mausolée
    Fa ny havanao e!
    No hilanja anao any amin'ny mausolée.

4. page 86. *"Dodo zaza! Dodo zaza!"*

5. page 87. *"Mpangala-jaza! Trimobe!"* Trimobé is an ogre in the tales and legends of Madagascar.

Moussa Diagana was born in M'Bout, Mauritania, in 1947. He is a sociologist educated at the University of Nouakchott, the University of Tunis, and the Sorbonne where he received his doctorate in 1981. A schoolteacher from 1969 to 1972, he worked on rural development projects in Mauritania from 1982 to 1989 and is now with the United Nations Development Program. His literary education began at the Nouakchott French Cultural Center in 1965 where he discovered the works of African and African-American writers such as Aimé Césaire, Amos Tutuola, Senghor, James Baldwin and Langston Hughes. He began writing short stories in primary school, poetry in high school, and plays in 1975. *The Legend of Wagadu* was written in 1985.

Richard Miller has translated many literary works of fiction and non-fiction, including several books by Brassai and Roland Barthes. He has translated five other plays published by Ubu Repertory Theater: Aimé Césaire's *A Tempest* (produced by Ubu in October 1991); Reine Bartève's *A Man With Women*; Sony Labou Tansi's *The Second Ark*, included in the anthology *Plays by Women*; and Jean-Marie Besset's *The Function*, included in the anthology *Gay Plays*. He also translated Jean-Marie Apostolidès' *Waiting for Beckett*, Michel Deutsch's *Thermidor*, Claire Etcherelli's *Germinal, Year III*, and, most recently, Jean-Marie Besset's *Fête Foreign*; all four plays were given staged readings at Ubu. Current translations include, among others, *Les pouvoirs de l'odeur*, by Annick Le Guerer, to be published by Random House next winter.

The premiere of the English translation of *The Legend of Wagadu as seen by Sia Yatabere* was directed in a staged reading by Dianne Kirksey-Floyd at Ubu Repertory Theater on April 29, 1991.

FOREWORD

Historically, the Empire of Ghana, or Wagadu (11th–13th centuries), described by Arab historians as the Land of Gold, included the southeastern part of Mauritania, a portion of Mali and the Senegalese "Fouta." The ruins of Kumbi, its capital, are to be found in south-eastern Mauritania.

Because of its rich gold deposits, Ghana was a center of trans-Saharan trade. Any gold, down to the tiniest nugget, discovered in the kingdom was the property of the Kaya Maghan, the King of Ghana. His subjects were allowed to keep any gold dust they might find. Contemporary Arab historians wrote of the wealth and luxurious spectacles of the Kaya Maghan's court. Succession was through maternal line.

The inhabitants of Ghana were pagan. They worshipped the Bida (a python), to which they made yearly sacrifices of a young female virgin. However, the Islamic faith was tolerated.

Kumbi, the capital, which is in the process of being excavated today, consisted of two cities: the royal city and the city of tradesmen and Arab caravaneers. The Arab sector of the city contained twelve mosques and there was one in the royal city. Some of the kingdom's dignitaries had converted to Islam.

In the 11th and 12th centuries Ghana was at war with the Almoravida, who wanted to convert the region to

Islam and control the trans-Saharan trade. Weakened by internal dissent, Ghana eventually fell to the Almoravida, who destroyed the capital.

The slow southward advance of desertification was another underlying reason for the decline of the Empire of Ghana, which began well before the Almoravidan conquest.

According to oral tradition, the Soninkes (founders of the Empire of Ghana) emigrated under the leadership of a man known as Din'ga. The problem was where they were to settle. A vulture and a hyena were consulted, and they indicated the site of Kumbi. The region was controlled by a huge black serpent with seven heads, the Bida. It allowed Din'ga and his people to settle in its lands with the proviso that each year they must present it with the most beautiful virgin in the land. They agreed to the bargain. Each year the Bida caused the rain to fall, and each year the inhabitants would collect the gold that had fallen at the time. The Soninkes called the land Wagadu (or Ghana), and the capital was called Kumbi.

One year, a girl named Sia Yatabere was chosen to be sacrificed to the Bida. Her fiancé, Mamadi Sefedan Kote (Mamadi the Silent) refused to allow it.

The Bida accepted the offerings made to him with three conditions: the girl must be a virgin, of noble blood and beautiful. Sia, who did not want to court dishonor, rejected her fiancé's urgings to flee and, despite her pleas, he then determined to save her by slaying the Bida.

He had a lance made by the best blacksmiths in Kumbi.

At dawn, as Sia was being led to the Bida's cavern,

Mamadi hid nearby and waited. When the Bida appeared, he fell upon it and cut off its seven heads (or the head regrew seven times and he cut it off each time). The last head raised its voice to the heavens and cried: "For seven years, seven months and seven days, not one drop of rain will fall on Wagadu, and you will never find another single nugget of gold."

Mamadi fled with the help of his uncle Wakhane Sakho, who gave him the fastest steed in Kaya Maghan's stables. He came to his mother's village, and she interceded with the people of Wagadu on his behalf. She proposed to feed them for seven years, seven months and seven days in exchange for her son's life. They decided not to kill Mamadi, but they rejected her proposal and went their separate ways. The legend concludes with an account of the love affair between Mamadi and Sia.

The legend "as seen by Sia Yatabere" follows neither the account written by historians nor the legend handed down by the *griots*. The first version is still incomplete and filled with gaps, and the second, like all myths, grows even dimmer with time. Each recounts a different tale, or perhaps they both tell the same story in different tongues.

We must rely on our imagination as we attempt to sort out and combine the two versions and to hear the voices of those men and women of the distant past who are so often ignored or forgotten, not to mention those men and women who, today, still wait vainly to see the green plains of Bambuk.

MOUSSA DIAGANA

CHARACTERS

SIA YATABERE
KAYA MAGHAN
WAKHANE SAKHO
MAMADI THE SILENT
KERFA THE FOOL
FIRST PRIEST
SECOND PRIEST
THIRD PRIEST
SIA YATEBERE'S FATHER
SIA YATEBERE'S MOTHER
KAYA MAGHAN'S GRIOT

CHIEF
ASSISTANT CHIEF } THE MASKED CHORUS
FLUNKY

When speaking as the MASKED CHORUS, *the* CHIEF, *the*
ASSISTANT CHIEF *and the* FLUNKY *don masks.*

SHACKLED CHORUS
BLIND CHORUS
MUTE CHORUS
KAYA MAGHAN'S COURT

THE PROLOGUE

THE MASKED CHORUS

CHIEF: Night is falling over Kumbi. Here and there, perhaps, curtains go up, life goes on . . .

ASSISTANT CHIEF: The whole panorama of life, the actors coming and going, perspiring and aspiring . . .

FLUNKY: . . . and eventually expiring . . .

CHIEF: . . . and you're becoming boring, Flunky, with all those unsuitable puns. We're here to talk about beginnings, not endings. I turn it over to you, Assistant Chief.

ASSISTANT CHIEF: We have actors appearing on the stage of life. Great and not-so-great, good and bad, famous and unknown. There are Kaya Maghan, Wakhane Sakho, as well as Mamadi the Silent, and Sia Yatabere . . . they need no introduction.

CHIEF: And then there are others, the nameless horde, those who drift along on the waves of that great river known as Time, which endures for eternity while they float on . . .

ASSISTANT CHIEF: . . . as colorless as indifference . . .

FLUNKY: . . . as transparent as poverty . . .

CHIEF: . . . as odorless as pain.

ASSISTANT CHIEF: As well as being barely presentable.

FLUNKY: Because of all the flies on their eyes and buzzing around them.

CHIEF: Their hands misshapen as their feet.

FLUNKY: And their tongues—they say that they're deadly poison.

CHIEF: In short, they're not really quite presentable . . . but present them we must. When the time comes, they'll make an appearance! And of course, as always, the usual precautions have been taken.

ASSISTANT CHIEF: Look, there, on the left, the Shackled Chorus. As their name indicates, their hands are shackled, but only at night. In the morning, it's their feet.

(*The* SHACKLED CHORUS *slowly crosses the stage.*)

CHIEF: That's to avoid any unpleasant complications. If they were unchained, they could walk on their hands and salute with their feet . . . Ladies and gentlemen, you don't seem to believe me! Show them, Flunky!

FLUNKY: Just the other day, Chief, they toed their noses at me.

CHIEF: Is that the best example you can give us, Flunky? You should be shackled too, since you do as much to me, whenever my back is turned.

FLUNKY: Wait, Chief, here's another one. Day-before-yesterday I disguised myself as a woman so as to get closer to them and hear what they were saying. Well, instead of trying to touch me you-know-where, they kicked me instead . . . you know where.

CHIEF: Bravo, Flunky! You're on the way to a promotion! Back to you, Assistant Chief. Continue with your introduction.

ASSISTANT CHIEF: Here, coming on from the right, we have the Blind Chorus. As their name would indicate, their eyes are blindfolded.

(*The* BLIND CHORUS *slowly crosses the stage.*)

CHIEF: Because of the flies that crawl around their eyes and buzz around them.

FLUNKY: Any back-up information needed here, Chief?

CHIEF: No. Go on, Assistant Chief.

ASSISTANT CHIEF: And last we have the Mute Chorus, who—as you will note—are wearing gags.

(*The* MUTE CHORUS *slowly crosses the stage.*)

FLUNKY (*to the audience*): Beware their tongues. Cut out their tongue, and it grows right back. The only solution is to gag them.

CHIEF: Yours will get the same treatment if you interrupt again when it's my turn to speak. The human refuse you have just seen pass by can be either good or evil, just as the waters of a river can be calm or rough.

ASSISTANT CHIEF: When the river's waters are calm, we call this human refuse "The Common Folk," for then they are well-behaved, they sing and dance in the moonlight. You can approach thém, but not too closely, of course, because of all the flies and everything.

CHIEF: And when the river's waters are rough, there are those who call them "The Mob." Those are the days when it's best not to get your feet wet.

ASSISTANT CHIEF: For if you do, you can be carried away like a piece of straw. Hold tight to the top of the tallest baobab tree, the one that stands farthest from the stream. Keep dry and wait for the waters to subside.

CHIEF: But for a while now, we haven't seen any human refuse float by. They're all waiting for something. Why are they waiting, Flunky? Why aren't they floating by on the stream as usual?

FLUNKY (wisely): Because the river is refusing to flow, Chief.

CHIEF: Not the river, you fool! History! Time! History has stopped advancing. It has stopped because the river has dried up. And do you know why the river has dried up, Flunky?

FLUNKY (*hesitantly*): Uh . . . because it's got holes in its bed, Chief . . . ?

CHIEF: Double fool! The holes you see in the riverbed are the wells the women have dug trying to find water. Yes, water, because it's been three years since a single drop of rain has fallen on Wagadu. The river has dried up. As a result, the human refuse is all backed up.

ASSISTANT CHIEF: As long as the river was flowing in its bed, as long as they could float along, good and evil, we could cope with things. But what can we do with refuse that doesn't float along, that just waits?

CHIEF: And, what's more, refuse that waits for news of flood or of fire, whichever: for either the refuse is consumed and the fire spreads or they are drowned and the river overflows its banks.

FLUNKY: In either case, Chief, the human refuse won't lose out, because soon they won't be refuse any longer and we may turn into it.

CHIEF: Well said, Flunky! You're beginning to make progress. (*To the audience*) So they wait and they hope.

FLUNKY: And what about us, Chief?

CHIEF: It's different with us. We're the masked chorus, the anonymous chorus . . .

ASSISTANT CHIEF: The faceless chorus . . .

FLUNKY: The coreless chorus . . .

CHIEF: Stop making those ridiculous puns, Flunky. Here, as everywhere, we have come among the people to listen to them, to learn what they're talking about, what they're thinking, what they're hiding, what they're plotting, and without anyone's knowing who we really are.

FLUNKY: You mean like spies . . .

CHIEF: Another unpleasant word! We are the Master's noble ears, his breath, his intuition . . . The moment is at hand. I can already hear the dogs barking. Come! To work. Assistant Chief, you go that way, and don't miss a word of what they say. You, Flunky, go over there, hide in that bush and try to find out what they're thinking. And don't forget, we'll meet at dawn back at the Master's to report.

ACT I

SCENE 1

THE FOOL

(*Kumbi Salé, capital of the Empire of Ghana. Night. In the
darkness we can make out a winding street lined with old
native houses. The silence is broken by the barking of dogs,
some of which break into loud howling when the* FOOL
*appears at the back of the alley. His hair is braided and filthy.
He carries a shepherd's crook and has a chain on one ankle.
The barking dies down gradually as he begins to speak. He
is nervous, his eyes are hollow and vacant, and as he speaks
he paces constantly back and forth.*)

FOOL: I greet you, people of Kumbi. Hail to thee, city of
Kumbi, city of a thousand lights! Hail to your opulence and your poverty, hail to your men and women,
noble and slave, dead and alive, I salute you!

Hail to you, Kaya Maghan, Master of the Universe.
Hear again the voice of Kerfa the Fool. The night
belongs to men's minds, the daytime to their deeds.
Awake, people of Kumbi, and hear me! I am called
Kerfa the Fool, but in truth I have neither name nor
age, and if anyone should ask you my purpose, tell
them that I am only passing through and that my
years are as many as the stones of the old city, as the
stones that the children of Kumbi cast at me as I go
by—my curses upon them and upon those who gave
them birth. For in truth I am the fiery word that
burns; in truth I am the gushing word that purifies,
the water that bears away.

Awake then, people of Kumbi, and you Priests of the Sacred Forest, dignitaries of the kingdom, and you too, Kaya Maghan! This world is not ruled by sleep, and what good is dying if we do not one day awake! Awake, if you would escape my words of fire and the waters that will bear you away. See how red the sky of Kumbi glows—the forecast is for showers of blood and tears.

Kaya Maghan! It is said that your kingdom knows no bounds, that it stretches from pole to pole, from the earth up to the heavens, from the rising to the setting sun. But I, Kerfa the Fool, I stand on the threshold of your words.

People of Kumbi! I am the thousand gusts of wind on the ocean of your orphan hopes, and my name is the ageless undertow that erodes the cliffs of the earth and then melts into the sea. If they ask you who I am, tell them that I am he who sees lightning and storms, he who hears the laughter of the starving hyena and the sobs of the thirsty jackal as they feed on the shaved skulls of your priests and the rounded flesh of your seven-fold accursed courtesans, and that my words of fire consume them and their waters bear them away.

Kaya Maghan! I am he who sees the empty bellies and the swarming flies in the vast cemetery where the corpses themselves dig their graves amid the whirling dust—dust of gold, gold and more gold! The walls of your palace gleam with gold, the spears of your warriors are tipped with gold, the bits of your horses are golden and they are shod with gold. A curse upon your gold, Kaya Maghan, and a curse upon your reign; may the sands of the desert bury your kingdom and may the blood of the thousand virgins sacrificed on the altar of the Wagadu-Bida rain upon your head. Ah, Wagadu-Bida, the god that devours his children, appear to me! I shall make you spit out your venom! Slimy and shapeless monster lurking in your fetid pit, what can you know of the sky and the stars, of the laughter of our maidens and the tears of our mothers?

People of Kumbi! The rain, the gold, the crops and the flocks of Wagadu are stained with blood. The ghoulish and stinking priests have chosen the loveliest daughter of Wagadu, but what do they know of beauty? All the daughters of Wagadu are beautiful, as are its sons, as are its trees.

And its wind. But the ghoul is drawn to the charnel house like the hyena to its feast. Go then, master-chefs of the Sacred Forest, and you, Kaya Maghan, high master of ceremonies, let the incestuous feast begin! There they are, like lovely frightened antelopes, silently grazing in the flickering shadows cast by the fires of your feast. Away! Away with the black sheep, away with the wild goats who have escaped the shepherd, who tear at our roots—away with them all!—so that your crops may grow and your lovely does may graze in peace, Kaya Maghan.

People of Kumbi, if they ask me who I am, tell them I am called Kerfa the Fool, but that I have neither name nor age. And tell them too, people of Kumbi, that I await below! At the edge of the great word, beyond the eternal city. There, I await you, not to sing your songs or keep time for your dances, but to accompany the deaf anger that suffuses your beings. Yes, I have awaited you below since the beginning, but even yesterday you still preferred the incestuous feast of Kaya Maghan, where you are made to sing loudly in order to drown out your own voices, where you are made to dance to still the impatience of your feet.

(The distant sounds of a drum are heard and gradually come nearer.)

Now the day is rising over Wagadu. I want deeds, not this imbecile sound of your evil drums. A curse upon you, people of Kumbi, with your sagging buttocks and your wobbly legs. I hate your songs and dances, but I tell you that the hyena does not dance and the vulture does not sing, and the wild dogs howl for death on Kumbi's hills.

So beat away, you drums, with skin stretched tight as corpses in the sun, blind drums, deaf drums, shackled and forgetful. Beat on, silent drums!

(The drums beat more and more loudly and drown out the FOOL's *voice as he covers his ears and goes off down the street, gesticulating.)*

Scene 2

KAYA MAGHAN

(The light gradually comes up on the stage as the drums continue to beat even more loudly. Male and female dancers set up the throne, lay the carpet and erect a canopy. One group of dancers takes up positions on either side of the throne as pages, while a second group becomes warriors bearing spears who form a guard of honor through whose ranks the dignitaries of the kingdom and priests of the Sacred Forest file to the foot of the throne. The priests wear white and have shaven heads; they stand opposite the dignitaries, who are dressed in luxurious bubus *with gold bracelets and necklaces; some have braided hair.* KAYA MAGHAN's GRIOT *stands at the side of the stage on which the priests, dignitaries, and later,* KAYA MAGHAN, *enter.)*

VOICE *(offstage)*: The Emperor of Wagadu! Kaya Maghan!

(The drums stop and a traditional guitar melody is heard

The VOICE *announcing* KAYA MAGHAN's *arrival draws nearer. Two girls enter, each bearing a vase containing burning incense. They take up positions on either side of the throne and silently to the back.*

KAYA MAGHAN *enters. His hair is braided and he is simply dressed. While the procession slowly advances to the throne and the honor guard take up positions in front of the two entrances to the stage, the* GRIOT *speaks.)*

THE GRIOT: The sun rises, the sun appears. The light is with us. Kaya Maghan, Master of Gold, Tunka of

110

Wagadu, may the evil eye be shut and the wicked tongue fall silent. Kaya Maghan yesterday, Kaya Maghan today, Kaya Maghan tomorrow. Thus goes the world. Oh Master of the Universe, the sun is your vestment and the rainbow your crown. Oh today's refuge, you are the memory of age-old yesterdays and of the eternal tomorrow. Shepherd of a thousand stars, you are the Keeper of the Word and the Master of Silence, you are the Eagle of the Skies. Your eye is the zenith and your splendor is over all. You are the Baobab of the Plain, the Shadow of the Spring and the Assuager of our Thirst. You are the Elephant of the Savannah, your gait is serene and your step is sure. N'Deysane! Master of the Heavens!

Your are the Man of Twelve-Thousand Clouds, Kaya Maghan yesterday, Kaya Maghan today, Kaya Maghan tomorrow: thus goes the world. Through your will I am but borrowed words, by the will of Wagadu-Bida, you are the Word itself.

People of Wagadu! The great day is come. Today calls forth all who remember yesterday and all who think of the morrow. It calls forth those bound by the Pact, by blood and water, by navel and milk. The sun rises, the sun is come, the sun is here. Kaya Maghan yesterday, Kaya Maghan today, Kaya Maghan tomorrow, thus goes the world, like gold dust, but dust no less, dust blown away on the wind.

(*As the* GRIOT *speaks the last words he strews gold dust in* KAYA MAGHAN'*s path. When the latter is seated on the throne, the* GRIOT *comes to stand on his right.*)

THE GRIOT: People of Kumbi! Kaya Maghan speaks. I, the Griot, son and grandson of the Griots of Kaya Maghan, am but a man of borrowed words. May my tongue be slit if it speaks other than what my ears shall hear, and let my ears be cut off if they hear other than the words of Kaya Maghan.

(KAYA MAGHAN *speaks. His voice is inaudible. His lips barely move. The* GRIOT, *in a loud voice, transmits his words to the court.*)

THE GRIOT: People of Kumbi, hearken to the words of Kaya Maghan: People of Wagadu, I salute you. I salute the seven priests of the Sacred Forest and their three envoys among us. I salute the dignitaries of my empire, the governors of my provinces and the war-chiefs of my armies . . . I salute the men and women of Kumbi, our living and our dead. Know ye that the great day is now come and that I swear upon my reign and upon my shroud that the Blood Pact will be respected so that Wagadu may live. Priests of the Sacred Forest, beseech Wagadu-Bida, our Snake-God, to help us to conquer our enemies . . . to protect us against ourselves, against man's selfishness, covetousness and neglect. May he impart to us the water from on high and the gold from beneath the earth, may he grant to us long life, and to our children, and may our grandchildren bury us. May he unite us daily more closely by navel and by milk.

(*aside*) By navel and milk! Thus goes the world! Now, Priests of the Sacred Forest, speak by the will of Kaya Maghan!

THE LEGEND OF WAGADU AS SEEN BY SIA YATABERE

FIRST PRIEST: By Din'ga, the ancestor that has fixed our path.

SECOND PRIEST: By the vulture and the hyena who have guided our steps.

THIRD PRIEST: By Wagadu-Bida who has given us shelter.

FIRST PRIEST: Remembrance is the root of the world.

SECOND PRIEST: Memory is its seed.

THIRD PRIEST: The sworn word is its fruit.

FIRST PRIEST: Bitter or sweet, the fruit is the fruit. It must be harvested and its seed sown so that the tree may spring up again and the seasons continue to turn.

THE THREE PRIESTS IN UNISON: Thus goes the world!

SECOND PRIEST: Kaya Maghan, the fruit is ripe.

SECOND PRIEST: And this world is not ours.

THIRD PRIEST: You have sown, we are but the harvesters.

FIRST PRIEST: We are but the messengers of the primal word.

SECOND PRIEST: Wagadu-Bida spake thus: She must be the most beautiful, and it must be so.

THIRD PRIEST: Wagadu-Bida spake thus: She must have noble blood, and it must be so.

FIRST PRIEST: Wagadu-Bida spake thus: She must be free from any stain, and it must be so.

SECOND PRIEST: Faithful to our given word, fate this year has chosen Sia of the clan of Yatabere.

THE GRIOT: Honor to their house and honor to the mother of Sia Yatabere! Blood does not perish, milk does not lie! Thus goes the world.

THIRD PRIEST: When the shadows of the night fall over Wagadu . . .

FIRST PRIEST: We shall come to seek Sia, daughter of Yatabere.

SECOND PRIEST: We shall lead her deep into the Sacred Forest.

THIRD PRIEST: She will wait by the cavern of Wagadu-Bida.

FIRST PRIEST: So that at dawn what has been spoken may be accomplished.

PRIESTS IN UNISON: Thus goes the world. Speak now the borrowed words. By the shadows that guide us and in which we are lost, speak them, Kaya Maghan.

THE GRIOT: Kaya Maghan speaks: Harken to the borrowed words. By my reign and my shroud, keep them, Priests of the Sacred Forest.

PRIESTS IN UNISON: We have heard the borrowed words. By Wagadu-Bida, our Snake God, who protects us from the world of the living, speak them, Kaya Maghan.

THE GRIOT: Kaya Maghan speaks: Harken to the borrowed words. By Wagadu-Bida, our Snake-God, who protects us from the world of the dead, I speak them. People of Wagadu! Hearken to the words of Kaya Maghan: What has been spoken will be accomplished. I, Kaya Maghan, will give to the father of Sia Yatabere the equal of his daughter's weight in gold. To Sia's mother will I give seven slaves of eighteen winters. Wakhane Sakho, inform your nephew, Mamadi the Silent, betrothed of Sia, that there are in Kumbi many other virgins of noble blood. Let him choose one of them, and I myself will tomorrow join them in marriage. Thus speaks Kaya Maghan, oh people of Kumbi. Now let us hear you, Yatabere, father of Sia.

YATABERE: My blood and the blood of my blood will flow with greater honor if such may give life to Wagadu.

THE COURT (*approvingly*): Ahan!

THE GRIOT: Thus goes the world! And now speak to us, Wakhane Sakho, Chief of the Armies and Police, uncle of Sia's fiancee.

WAKHANE SAKHO: Oh Kaya Maghan, my nephew, Mamadi Sefedan Kote, will be proud of the honor you have done him, even if it takes many winters to extinguish his burning passion for Sia Yatabere. At the moment he is leading his men in battle against the Almoravida on the cliffs of Awdaghost. I shall see that he returns this very evening to Kumbi to gaze upon Sia once again.

THE GRIOT: Kaya Maghan speaks: Is the return of Mamadi the Silent really necessary? Is his presence on the battlefield not more important? What is the mind of the leader of my armies?

WAKHANE SAKHO: I do not believe that we can tear the betrothed of Mamadi the Silent from him without allowing him to . . .

FIRST PRIEST: Who speaks of "tearing from him"? This man blasphemes, Kaya Maghan! He must retract his words! We are not beggars, we seek no benefit, we are merely seeking our due. To whom does beauty, nobility and purity belong, if not to the Master of the Primal Word?

THE COURT (*approvingly*): Ahan!

WAKHANE SAKHO: I cannot retract what I have said, for I have not blasphemed, and you seem to have forgotten that eighteen winters ago my own daughter was sacrificed to the Snake God.

THE COURT: (*in approval of* WAKHANE SAKHO'*s speech*): Ahan!

SECOND PRIEST: You are right, we *had* forgotten. And why should we remember it? Here we see man's selfishness, this man's selfishness! We only take what we have lent; for that, we give him prosperity and peace, and he is asking us to be grateful to *him*! Oh Kaya Maghan, Sia, daughter of Yatabere, now belongs to the Wagadu-Bida, and no man has the right to look upon her.

THE COURT (*approving his words*): Ahan!

WAKHANE SAKHO: Sia is still in Kumbi and Kumbi is not the Sacred Forest; so long as she is not within the Sacred Forest, the living still have a right to look upon her.

THE COURT (*approving*): Ahan!

THIRD PRIEST: Sacrilege! The Sacred Forest, Kumbi, all Wagadu and you yourself—all belong to the Snake God. This man insults us, oh Kaya Maghan, he insults the Wagadu-Bida, he insults all the people of Wagadu, our people!

WAKHANE SAKHO: And what of the people! What do you know about them, you who do not dwell among us, who are not of our world?

FIRST PRIEST: Nor are the souls of man of this world, and Wakhane Sakho is forgetting that we are the souls of the people.

WAKHANE SAKHO: And you are forgetting that the people have more than one soul. They have a stomach that grows hungrier each day, they have feet that grow more and more tired of following you, they have hearts that no longer beat with love for you.

SECOND PRIEST: Because men like you are slowly working away to undermine us and to corrupt the people's hearts and soil their souls.

WAKHANE SAKHO: Let Kaya Maghan be my judge. I am the Leader of his armies and police, and it is my duty to report to him what I know of his people. I speak only what is, even if the truth may cause you pain. No one is in a better position to know what the people think or what they mutter amongst themselves than am I. Oh Kaya Maghan, it has been three years since a drop of rain has fallen in Wagadu. Your rivers are dry, your pastures have turned to sand and your flocks are decimated. Even your army fights without conviction against the advancing Almoravida. The sons of Wagadu are perishing by the hundreds on the cliffs of Awdaghost, and your people are beginning to wonder what all those sacrifices have achieved.

FIRST PRIEST: They will have been to no avail for you perform them grudgingly, with angry hearts! Oh Kaya Maghan, some of your subjects here within the court have betrayed our faith and gone over to Islam. They conspire day and night against the sun of the Snake God. They desire our deaths, and yours as well. *They* are the cause of the wrath of the Snake God and of the misfortunes that have befallen Wagadu.

WAKHANE SAKHO: I do not keep the people's soul, but I know that the people are not going over to Islam, even though their anger is growing by the day. Soon, I shall bring you proof. Oh Kaya Maghan, they are tired of waiting in vain for water from the heavens. They want to leave, they want to move south to the green plains of the Bambuk . . .

SECOND PRIEST: All lies! The people believe in us, we know it. But some of your subjects present here are urging them to emigrate to the Bambuk to make them forget their gods. We will never leave here, not even if Kumbi should be destroyed utterly. The sanctuary of the Wagadu-Bida is here, this is the resting place of Din'ga and of all our ancestors. To leave would mean abandoning our memory, to leave would destroy our seed and deprive us of any resting place at our deaths.

WAKHANE SAKHO: I am only reporting what the people are thinking, and whatever may happen, I will be the last to leave Kumbi. But having said that, Mamadi the Silent has been at the front for two years now, and I still think that, as we take from him today what we . . . lent him yesterday, we have a duty to allow him to look upon her for one last time. A messenger stands ready to take him the news. I ask for your decision, oh Kaya Maghan.

THE GRIOT: Kaya Maghan speaks: As for what the people are saying and thinking, all in good time. As for the Pact that brings us together at this place today, Sia, daughter of Yatabere, belongs to the Wagadu-Bida, for the mouths of the priests speak truth. As for Wakhane Sakho, his words too are just, even though he has spoken more as the uncle of Mamadi the Silent

119

then as the Leader of my armies. Let Mamadi the Silent remain where he is. He will be informed after the sacrifice has been made.

THE COURT (*approving*): Ahan!

WAKHANE SAKHO: Thy will be done, oh Kaya Maghan!

THE GRIOT: What has been spoken shall be accomplished. Thus goes the world. Now, Wakhane Sakho, speak to us again on the other subject for today.

(*At a signal from* WAKHANE, *two warriors enter escorting the* FOOL *his hands bound.*)

WAKHANE SAKHO: Behold the man, oh Kaya Maghan, he whose words have disturbed all Kumbi. He claims to be speaking on behalf of some unknown power. He drags all of Wagadu in the mud—the people of Kumbi, the high officials of the Empire, Kaya Maghan himself and even the Wagadu-Bida, (*Addressing the priests, ironically*) and even, alas, upon the priests of the Sacred Forest, whom he calls old hyenas with stinking breath. All Kumbi listens to him because he also claims to be the people's shepherd and savior, and all look forward to his nightly appearances. Unrest grows among your people, and this man is partly responsible. (*Shoving the* FOOL *forward*) On your knees before the justice of Kaya Maghan!

FOOL (*rising*): They hate my words and so they whip my back to bloody ribbons. They are afraid of my words and so they bind my hands. Is this your justice, oh

Kaya Maghan! Is it so base that I must put myself on its level by kneeling?

WAKHANE SAKHO (*To the warriors*): Strike him! Strike this man who insults the justice of Kaya Maghan! Break his feet! On your knees . . . force him to kneel!

(KAYA MAGHAN *raises his hand and stops them as they are about to obey.*)

THE GRIOT: Kaya Maghan speaks: Stop, do not touch this man. Kaya Maghan speaks: My justice is great enough to control this man. Let him stand. My justice has leveled more than one baobab. Let him stand and let him speak.

FOOL: Domination is not victory, oh Kaya Maghan, and baobabs have never withstood the wind for long. And that is what your justice is: wind!

(KAYA MAGHAN *again makes a gesture and stops the warriors who are preparing to strike the* FOOL *on orders from* WAKHANE SAKHO.)

FOOL: So let me be judged! What a pitiful group of men you have here, pretending to control the fate of a whole people while from dawn to dusk they spend their time calmly plotting to send a young girl to her death. I have traveled as far as the borders of the Bambuk, and to the Bouré, and wherever I have gone, water has come from the sky, gold has come from the water, hearts have been filled with peace—

and all the treasures of the world are not worth the life of one young girl. So let me be judged! Death? What are you waiting for? Inflict it upon me! What else do you know how to do, you and the accursed creature you call your Snake God?

THE THREE PRIESTS (*trembling with indignation*): Enough! Enough! He goes too far! He blasphemes and insults us!

FIRST PRIEST: Oh Kaya Maghan, this is due to you! We no longer have any place here! We have allowed this man to speak and night after night to insult the Wagadu-Bida throughout Kumbi and even in the midst of your court! (*looking at* WAKHANE SAKHO) You allow those who are secret moslems to sow discord amongst your people and to conspire against your power and to question our faith. Beware the wrath of the Snake God, oh Kaya Maghan, and beware the apocalypse that awaits your kingdom.

FOOL: Let the apocalypse come, then, and let it destroy you all, your crimes, your greed and the shameful business you call the Blood Pact. If the religion you call Islam can wipe you out, then let it do so, and welcome to it! One day the truth will prevail over your eight hundred years of lies!

WAKHANE SAKHO: Now you know this man, this vermin who is corrupting the souls and the hearts of your people by preaching revolt. We await your judgment, oh Kaya Maghan.

THE GRIOT: Kaya Maghan speaks: I have heard this man's words. If words are fire, it is the mouth that utters them that will burn, not the ear that hears them. People of Wagadu, no blood will be spilled today but the blood of sacrifice. Thus, I, Kaya Maghan, decree that tonight this man will speak as usual to the people of Kumbi, to urge them to repent and to ask forgiveness from the Snake God. Should he fail to do so, I will deliver him into the hands of the priests of the Sacred Forest so that tomorrow what has been spoken may be accomplished. People of Kumbi, Kaya Maghan asks forgiveness for your pain. He thanks you and he asks that Wakhane Sakho remain behind. To the rest of you, Kaya Maghan bids you to share with him this evening, beneath the thousand lanterns of his palace, the repose of peace in navel and in milk. Thus goes the world!

(*The drums beat. As the stage empties,* WAKHANE SAKHO *approaches* KAYA MAGHAN *and speaks to him. As soon as the two men are alone,* WAKHANE SAKHO *appears to be upset and begins to pace up and down.*)

WAKHANE SAKHO: Without wishing to disobey you, oh Kaya Maghan, what you ask is impossible. You and this man! You don't know the danger you are risking! You must have seen that he's a raving lunatic! He might make some move against your person, or worse; who can tell? If you wish him to repent, leave that up to me. I have many ways of making him do that! But believe me, your person is too precious for us to risk . . . And I am responsible for your safety. What would I say to the Wagadu should anything happen to you? Or let me be present at your meeting . . . Think on it, oh Kaya Maghan . . .

KAYA MAGHAN: Wakhane Sakho, do you imply that I take decisions without thinking? Bring this man to me and leave us alone.

(WAKHANE SAKHO *hesitates for a moment and then goes to the exit and calls in the two warriors escorting the* FOOL.)

KAYA MAGHAN: Untie this man and go.

(WAKHANE SAKHO *hesitates again, opens his mouth as if to speak, restrains himself and then exits with the two warriors, leaving* KAYA MAGHAN *alone with the* FOOL. *The latter stands at the far left of the stage with a blank stare and does not seem aware of* KAYA MAGHAN's *presence.* KAYA MAGHAN *observes him for a long moment.*)

KAYA MAGHAN: I will call you Kerfa since that is what the people of Kumbi call you. I have had you brought here because I want to save your life.

FOOL: By asking me to croak louder than the frogs when darkness falls that Kaya Maghan is great and that the Wagadu-Bida is our generous benefactor? What will you be saving me from? The wrath of the hyenas? The venom of your subjects?

KAYA MAGHAN: On the contrary, I want you to speak as you spoke yesterday and the day before that, as you have always spoken, but I want you to do so in the full light of day.

FOOL: You have made yourself the sun, Kaya Maghan, and when your rays burn men's words where can they hide save in the shadows? I do not want your sun, Kaya Maghan, my words will illuminate even those eyes blinded by your daylight.

KAYA MAGHAN: As you say, Kerfa. I have been made into a sun, and the glare of my own rays blinds me as well. A blind sun seeking a ray of light imprisoned in the night. Such am I. Speak for me too, Kerfa.

FOOL: Never, Kaya Maghan! I shall speak, but against you, for there is no place for your sun in my darkness. Rise in the east, set in the west, but know that you cannot enter the realm of darkness.

KAYA MAGHAN: Kerfa, the rays of my sun cannot even light its own way, or perhaps they have blinded me and I cannot see it—what does it matter. You alone can shed new light on the truth of things, the truth of everyday. Speak so that together we can voice the truth about my people.

FOOL: Do you seek a voice? Two thousand voices are raised each day at the foot of your throne. The voices of the griots, the voices of priests, the voices of warriors, the voices of councilors, all are raised beneath your sun. What do you have to complain about?

KAYA MAGHAN: About the sea of complacency that drowns me. You have said it: the laughter of the starving hyenas, the venom of snakes, the shrieking of thirsty jackals, the ceremonial words. I pay, and in return I am given two thousand honeyed words. I chastise, and as many tongues lick my feet. I am tired of it, Kerfa. I am tired of the ever-more worldly priests of the Sacred Forest, I am tired of all the squabbling and petty backbiting of my chameleon-like officials with their multi-hued ambitions, of the bad advice of ignorant councilors who seek only to curry favor. I am tired of the sound of my own voice, even of my silences, and of the echoes of my words in the speeches of the griots, of all the Kaya Maghans of yesterday, today and tomorrow, tired of this world that I would like to see different. Would that it might finally change, and that our hopes might be realized. I want to drive away all the pecking, clucking fowl that deafen me so that I hear the voice of my people. Am I not king? I am Kaya Maghan! So return my people to me! I want to meet them, Kerfa, and you are the only one who can show me the way.

FOOL: Listen carefully, Kaya Maghan. Can you not hear the muffled sound that rises from the depths of Kumbi into the very heart of your palace? Listen . . .

KAYA MAGHAN: I have listened so often, Kerfa, but I can hear no sound, no complaint. You know how thick the walls of my palace are.

FOOL: Then open wide the doors and let in the howling mob.

KAYA MAGHAN: No! I want to go to my people before they come to me. Where are my people, Kerfa? Who are they, what are they saying?

FOOL: Ha! Ha! Ha! Kaya Maghan is looking for his people! The brave shepherd seeks his sheep! You want to know where your people are? Well then, Kaya Maghan: they are wherever you are not. You want to know who your people are? Your people are no more. They have become what you have made them, a spell in the mouth of the Griot. You want to know what they are saying? Ha! Ha! Ha! The words of the people! They're like a king's fart, everyone can smell it, but everyone must pretend not to have heard it! The delicate odor of a king's fart! Ha! Ha! Ha!

KAYA MAGHAN (*raising his voice*): And you, then—where are *your* people hiding, and who are you to speak on their behalf, when you heap insults upon them?

FOOL: I dream dreams for others. My people? I have no people—or, at least, not yet. So why should I respect yours, the howling mob, out for its own blood? Today they dance in your sunlight, tomorrow they'll trample you in the dust to praise a different tyrant, following the insane beat of their accursed drums: with empty bellies, yet still laughing hysterically—those are your people, Kaya Maghan! Your people are accursed, and I am tired, Kaya Maghan. Innocence has even vanished from the souls of the children. They cast stones at me and mock my madness. And yet they know I have no name and that I am as old as the stones of this ancient city. I shun sleep, Kaya Maghan, and yet their dreams seek me out, they overwhelm me and assail the defenses of my madness. I am tired of dying with each dawn, since life is a tempting poison. I am afraid, Kaya Maghan, afraid of the cold intelligence that sometimes pierces through my folly. Kaya Maghan! you seek your people and I seek myself. Where is he who has nor name nor age? At what crossroads will my dreams come to fruition?

(*He falls to his knees, sobbing.*)

KAYA MAGHAN (*Approaching the* FOOL, *he takes him by the shoulders and lifts him.*): I cannot see my people, and yours do not hear you. Can we not join forces? Let us join day and night. You will lend me your eyes and I will raise a thousand monuments for your words. Join your shepherd's crook to my scepter, your tresses to my crown, and we will cleave the wind and free the light that lies below the shadows. (*He releases the* FOOL *and moves downstage.*) I have commanded a thousand brushfires to keep my people wakeful and to dispel the shadows from my kingdom. I want men to dream beneath my sun, Kerfa, and I appoint you Grand Master of Waking Dreams and Minister of Hope. This year shall be the year of dream—let it be spoken throughout Wagadu! Let a thousand schools be created and let all our children be taught hope! Order the treasurer of my kingdom to raise a monument to the glory of dreams, a monument that will rest upon the rainbow of my crown! I want streams of honey for all the orphans of Wagadu, I want milk to rain down upon them. For each woman of Wagadu I want a name, and their symbol to be the turtle dove, mistress of the wind. Soldiers, turn your spears into torches to light our future defeats. Let them beat the *djoubouré* and dance the *worosso* at the gates of our cemeteries. (*Taking the* FOOL *by the hand*) Sit upon my throne,

Kerfa, and dream! I will raise up the wind, I will travel faster then time and I will bring your words to the seven borders of Wagadu! Drums! (*The drums begin to beat.*)

FOOL (*coming to himself suddenly, with anger*): No! Never, Kaya Maghan! Never, do you hear? My dreams cannot be confined and penned up by your blind geometry. I reject your bargain. I've told you: your kingdom is not mine: keep your sun for yourself. (*Suddenly struck with an idea, he thinks a moment and then speaks sarcastically.*) Or no—we *will* make a deal . . . we'll hold an auction, and all of Wagadu will be present. (*gesturing, as if addressing a large crowd*) Step right up, my good people, step right up! We're going to have an auction! For three empty stomachs, Kaya Maghan is offering a courtier's paunch! What am I bid? Going . . . going . . . there, on the left, did I hear someone offer a tubercular cough? Bravo! That's three empty stomachs and a tubercular cough for a courtier's fat gut . . . Going . . . going . . . There, on the right, a nubile young girl's body? Wonderful! For a courtier's gut . . . there, the blood of one virgin!

KAYA MAGHAN: Enough! Your madness is not for sale, I know. I want to give it meaning . . .

FOOL: Ah! So that's what it is . . . a meaning to my madness. Why not start with giving some meaning to your power?

KAYA MAGHAN: Now we're talking. A meaning to my power? What power has meaning in the eyes of the

people? And what do you know about power, Kerfa?
You talk about it night and day, and your words are
fine words, but I live it. I act, and there's no salvation
in acts. When I raise armies to defend our homes I'm
called a vampire, a killer of children! When I store up
today's harvest for tomorrow's crops, I am starving
the people. When I open wide the doors of light, I am
nothing but an enlightened despot. If I am the
noonday sun, I burn your eyes, if I begin to set, I do
not shed enough light to light your cottages. And
what do people whisper to each other when I feed my
subjects with my own hands? "Ah," they say, "Kaya
Maghan is trying to ration every mouthful of food we
eat!" Were I to wash their feet they would mutter that
I'm afraid they'll soil the carpets in my palace. Kerfa,
give *me* the everyday, *you* take time itself, and together
we will have an eternity. Why do you refuse to act
with me?

FOOL: When the children of Kumbi throw their stones,
Sia binds my wounds, when I've walked all night she
offers me a place to rest my tired feet, and when I lose
hope she is there to dry my tears. But you, Kaya
Maghan, you not only feed Sia to the Snake God, but
you bid all the people dance and sing at the gates of
your palace. That is your everyday. And my time is
the bitter taste of the blood of all the murdered Sias
that I must drink down to the dregs.

KAYA MAGHAN: That everyday will cease to be, and you
must forget those days. Together, we must forge a
new eternity. One that will give meaning to our deeds,
to our impatient nights, to the anxiety with which we

awaken. I know . . . that the sun of the Snake God is slowly setting in the ocean of our sufferings. I am a shepherd too, Kerfa, and I can sense the impending storm. I want to collect our flock as quickly as I can and keep them safe for another sun, for other pastures, for less bloody sacrifices. Only you can help me do this.

FOOL: If the sun of Wagadu-Bida is setting, so much the better! Men say that the new sun of Islam is about to rise in the East. Why not embrace that religion and use it to create the new eternity you seek?

KAYA MAGHAN: Because our people will not follow me. At any rate not today, for they have not heard the new message. But they do know yours. I know that at my court there are those who *have* converted to Islam and who are plotting against my crown. The enemies of Wagadu are rallying to it. My conversion would only bring me down more quickly and distance me still farther from my people. Time passes so quickly, Kerfa, and a people who no longer believe in their own eternity are a dead people.

FOOL: Go then! Go deep into the Sacred Forest and dig your grave, Kaya Maghan, for this vile world holds nothing more for you.

KAYA MAGHAN: I still have you, Kerfa, your dreams, your madness, the last, the true refuge of our eternity, the one that comes from the people, since you are another us. You are the people's broken heart, its tired legs, its stifled voice. I am only Kaya Maghan, alone in my power. Give me your hand, Kerfa, let us go down together into the old city and speak. Tell them Kaya Maghan has answered your call and let us all set out together on the final voyage. If you wish Sia to live, let us travel up the river to its source to find the spring, the pure water of our eternity.

FOOL: All the Sias of Wagadu are dead and the waters of the primal spring are scarlet with their blood. Lift your head, Kaya Maghan, and look at the moon. That is the people you seek. For you, the visible smiling face, singing and dancing; for me, the side with the hidden face, the one you will never see, the one that moans, distorted, a thorn in its limping foot. My people are not your people, Kaya Maghan, and I want to lead mine along other paths and toward future horizons without you, Kaya Maghan, for you are already dead. Dead in the breast of every murdered virgin, dead in every mother's womb. (*Still speaking, he exits slowly.*) Kaya Maghan has been dead from the beginning, extinguished by his own sun. Kaya Maghan is dead! Hear me, people of Kumbi! The king is dead, long live the fool!

ACT II

Scene 1

Sia Yatabere
The Noon-Day Queen

(The interior of the Yataberes' house, with a courtyard. Sia, seated on a stool, is working at a spinning wheel. Kerfa enters, ignoring her, sits down with a calabash and begins to eat hungrily.)

SIA (*without looking up*): Ah, so you're back at last. Your dinner is probably cold by now.

(There is a long pause.)

SIA: Kerfa, do you know I'm going to die at dawn? (*pause*) You must have heard by now, you know everything that happens in Kumbi. Doesn't it spoil your appetite at all? You must be truly famished. You seem even hungrier than usual today.

FOOL (*with his mouth full, in between bites, and without looking at her*): I've got to eat twice as much as usual today because if you're going to die tomorrow evening there won't be anyone to save some food for me.

SIA (*half in jest, half in earnest*): So, enjoy it! You really ought to eat a lot more, as well, for the day after, and the day after that . . .

FOOL: After tomorrow, I'll be dead.

SIA (*sarcastic*): Are you going to kill yourself because of me?

FOOL: In a way . . . with the help of Kaya Maghan and his priests. Their Pact prevents them from spilling any blood but yours on the day of sacrifice. So your death gives me an extra day—for which I thank you.

SIA: You'd best take your time eating, then, because where we're going everything must be eaten cold. (*long pause*) They say that Kaya Maghan received you all alone in his palace. What did he want?

FOOL: To save us both from death.

SIA: Save us from death? What about the animal sacrifice? What about your sentence? Has he lost his mind?

FOOL: Not yet, but he's trying. Unfortunately, it's not as easy as you might think. He's a politician . . . he knows that the people are right but that the world can no longer be governed by right alone. And he's a strategist—he'll send us to die in order to use our lives as bargaining chips. He wants my madness and my dreams to govern . . .

SIA: So we're saved!

FOOL (*not listening and continuing to eat*): He wants to turn things around and to get rid of his priests, his councilors, the whole bunch of them, as he says, and reach out to the people before the people come after him to throw him out . . .

SIA: Kerfa, answer me! Did you agree? Will our lives be spared?

FOOL (*not listening*): Kaya Maghan wants to travel up the river, but we're nearing the falls, the current is strong, the winds are against us . . .

SIA: Kerfa! Answer me! What did you decide to do?

FOOL (*not listening*): Since he cannot travel against the current, Kaya Maghan would like to turn his people into a thousand hippopotamuses with their snouts stuck in the mud so that he can then walk across their backs to the river's source.

SIA: If I understand what you're saying, then, you refused his offer? Kerfa, answer me!

KERFA (*ignoring her*): He's going to the river's source to purify himself, not to save the people. Sia, the people's safety is at stake, and Kaya Maghan wants to . . .

SIA (*rising angrily*): What do I care what Kaya Maghan wants! I want to live, I don't care how! Why did you refuse him, Kerfa? Why? I want to live, do you hear? Live!

FOOL (*beginning to laugh*): And here I thought that girls in Wagadu were so fond of compliments! I guess I'll never understand women! You do one of them the honor of selecting her as the most beautiful girl in Wagadu and she gets all upset! Ha, ha, ha!

SIA: That's one compliment I can do very well without, thank you! (KERFA *continues to laugh.*) And it's nothing to laugh about, either! You're heartless!

FOOL (*ignoring her*): And what have they always done? The men, I mean. They look for the most beautiful ewe in the flock—and they always manage to find one. The one with the softest fleece, the tenderest flesh. And then they take their sharpest knife and gently caress her throat with it, and the ewe's throat turns red and her blood gushes out. Think of it—what an honor for a mere sheep, to know that on the day she's sacrificed she's the most beautiful one in the flock!

SIA: I'm not a sheep, Kerfa. I'm a woman. A woman who wants to live! Kerfa, look at me! I have a woman's heart, a woman's breasts . . . Save me from death! All you can think about is the people—think about me, too, me, Sia Yatabere. I don't want to die!

FOOL (*not listening*): Beneath the soft, thick wool its tender flesh quivers at the man's touch. The blade caresses her slowly before it makes it sudden slash. Her back stiffens, she struggles to free herself from the tight embrace in which he holds her, her eyes turn up, she goes into a final spasm and then her last gasp . . . And then death. Pleasure or plain—what does it matter? To die while the blood of her lost virginity still flows . . .

(*He falls to the ground face down with a hoarse cry and then begins to sob.* SIA *goes to him, kneels beside him and cradles his head in her arms.*)

FOOL (*sobbing*): Tell me again that you're not that sheep, Sia . . . that you're a woman who wants to live . . . to go on living.

SIA: Let them call me Sia daughter of Yatabere if they like, but I am a woman of Wagadu, a woman without age, a woman without a name. Woman. A woman who bears their children, whose back is bent from carrying their burdens. But now, tonight, I want to stand upright and say No! No to my father! No to my mother! No to my man! From now on, my only offspring will be my repressed anger. I've been killed enough. Tonight, I want to live again!

(*Both rise and each speaks in soliloquy*)

FOOL: They have arrayed you in gold from head to toe.

SIA: My steps are slow, my gestures weighty.

FOOL: For you they have build a thousand castles.

SIA: Their walls were high and their dungeons deep.

FOOL: They have set you upon a pedestal.

SIA: Merely a silent statue, impervious to time.

FOOL: They have subjected you to their passions.

SIA: Passions that defile my heart.

FOOL: A heart greater than their minds.

SIA: Their minds confined in a sheep's brain. But the sheep is dead, long live the woman! Let Kaya Maghan and his gold be borne away on the raging flood, but I will live.

FOOL (*suddenly returning to reality*): Sia, do you know the legend?

SIA: What legend, Kerfa?

FOOL: The legend of Wagadu. The one the griots will one day tell the children of Wagadu.

SIA: What does the legend say, Kerfa?

FOOL (*as if addressing an imaginary audience, half serious, half in jest*): In that year the young virgin Sia of the clan of Yatabere was chosen from among the noblest and most beautiful maidens of Wagadu to be sacrificed to the Wagadu-Bida. When he heard the news, her betrothed, Mamadi the Silent, hastened to her dwelling, his heart filled with rage, and begged her to flee with him beyond the mountains of Bouré to the green plains of Bambuk. Anywhere. Away. He wanted to remove her from the kingdom of the Snake God. Sia heard him out, standing tall and proud. In her veins flowed the blood of the Yatabere, and a Yatabere does not fear death. "I have always said yes to you, Mamadi," she said, "but today I must say no. I will not run from death." And Mamadi continued to plead with her, but to no avail. As night fell, the priests of the Sacred Forest came to fetch her and led her to the cavern of the Snake God.

(He breaks off and turns slowly to SIA*)*

SIA: And then? Go on! I want to know! What does the legend say?

FOOL: You'll find out in the last act. When all is accomplished—if you're still alive.

SIA: Believe me, Kerfa, women have always been able to get around legends. I'll be alive. But I still don't see Mamadi the Silent. They say that the priests of the Sacred Forest have forbidden him to see me again. Will he come? I want to see him.

FOOL: He'll come. But in the meantime here are your parents. *(Sia's father and mother appear.)*

SIA *(speaking into* KERFA's *ear)*: And what does the beautiful legend of Wagadu have to say about my father and mother?

FOOL: Oh, it leaves them out. What's so important about a father and mother? A chance encounter . . . So you can do whatever you want with them, the story won't contradict you.

(Sia's parents move toward her. Her mother throws herself weeping into her daughter's arms.)

FATHER: Dry your tears, woman! Our sorrow is great indeed, but we must feel pride in giving our blood so that Wagadu may live.

(*The mother cries even harder.*)

FATHER (*angrily*): Stop crying, woman! Don't you realize that you are making your daughter even more unhappy, that you're making her lose courage?

MOTHER: What do I care about her courage, Yatabere? What do I care about the blood of the Yatabere when my daughter is about to die . . .

FATHER: You too will die. We will all die one day. But Sia's death is not like the others . . .

MOTHER: I know, and my sorrow isn't like other sorrows. I'm losing my daughter, my only hope, my only ray of light . . .

FATHER: For the grandeur of Wagadu, for the nobility of our blood!

MOTHER: I don't understand all those things, Yatabere. But if that's all it is, I'm going to see Kaya Maghan and his priests. Let them sacrifice me, but let them hear a mother's prayer and let my child live . . .

FATHER: Silence, madwoman! You don't know what you're saying.

SIA (*pushing her mother away*): Yes, mother, you don't know what you're saying. Father is right. I'm the one who was chosen, not you. Look at yourself, with your wrinkled face, your dried up skin, your bent back. Look at your thin white hair, your bitter mouth, the few yellowed teeth the years have left you. You're useless to them now. Even their death no longer needs you. I'm the one who was chosen, and do you know why? (*She moves toward her father suggestively*). Look at me, Father, and Mother will know why I've been chosen. (*She rips the top of her blouse and reveals her breasts*) Look at these young breasts, firm and warm as corn cake. (*She takes her father's hand and places it on her breast*) Touch them, caress them, feel how soft they are. Squeeze them in your hand! Am I not your blood, am I not yours, all yours? Take me!

MOTHER (*horrified*): Sia, my daughter, what are you doing? Are you forgetting that you're speaking to your father?

SIA: And my smooth body, see how plump and juicy it is. (*She spreads her legs.*) Look at my slender, taut legs, my soft, voluptuous thighs, my body just waiting for my virginal blood to flow . . .

MOTHER (*still weeping*): Sia!

SIA: Come on! I'm only a woman like all the rest, another sheep—even if I am the most beautiful! So come on, chief ram of the Yatabere, do with me as you have with that woman there you've squeezed dry like a lemon, bled dry, milked dry, emptied of sweat and tears. Isn't it my turn now? Come! I long to feel your sharp blade cut through my fleece. (*She falls sobbing to the ground.*) I long to cry out in pleasure . . . or in pain! I want to die as I have lived: at your hand! (*She falls silent and weeps silently.*)

MOTHER (*kneeling beside her and cradling her head in her arms*): Sia, my child . . .

SIA (*rising and repulsing her mother*): Don't touch me! If that's the man who fathered me, I don't want to be anyone's daughter.

FATHER: Kaya Maghan has done us the honor of agreeing to see us this evening, this woman and I. Since that's your attitude, I shall tell him that you shun death and that I renounce you.

SIA: I am no longer your daughter, Yatabere, and any honor is mine! As for death, I do not shun it. I agree to be sacrificed, but on one condition.

FATHER: Speak. I will promise you anything you want.

SIA: Tell Kaya Maghan that in exchange for my body he has promised this woman who calls herself my mother seven eighteen-year-old slaves, and that that is too much: I am worth no more than one. Tell him also that I thank him for the gift he has bestowed upon you of my weight in gold, and that my only regret is that you didn't fatten me up a little more.

FATHER (*shocked*): Sia! What are you trying to make me say! I could never speak to him like that! You're trying to humiliate us . . . we'll be the laughingstock of Wagadu. Anyway, I don't want the gold.

SIA: You'll take it, I'm worth it. And you will also tell him what I told you, or I'll withdraw my promise.

FATHER (*after a moment's hesitation*): Very well! I'll pass along your message, I'll accept the gold and I'll distribute it to the poor of Kumbi.

SIA: You can do what you want with it. Isn't that what you've done with me?

FATHER (*aside*): Great gods, what is this world coming to? Is it really my own blood speaking like this? (*to* SIA) We must go now. But we will return to watch with you until the priests arrive.

SIA: I want to be alone.

MOTHER: Sia, my poor child. Let me hold you in my arms, let me hold you close . . . please, just one last time . . .

SIA: No. Go, both of you. I've told you, I no longer belong to anyone.

MOTHER (*weeping*): No, I can't leave you. But I must see Kaya Maghan . . . I must speak to him.

FATHER (*pulling her away brutally*): Come away! We must not keep Kaya Maghan waiting.

(*They exit. The sound of the* MOTHER's *sobs can be heard offstage.*)

FOOL: The poor mother, who has nothing but her own death to offer in exchange for her daughter's life. Ha, ha! As if she lived . . .

SIA (*as if suddenly waking, rubbing her eyes and looking dazed*): Who said that? Is it you, Kerfa? And my parents . . . where are they? Why aren't they here yet?

FOOL: They were here, with you. They have left.

SIA: My mother and father were here? I can't remember! I can't remember anything . . . and why am I half naked? My clothes . . . why are they torn? Kerfa, I feel so tired . . . so . . . What has happened? Tell me, Kerfa . . . What happened? I can remember nothing.

FOOL: Sia, no legend in the world would dare relate what has happened.

SIA: But what did I say? What did I do? I have this strange feeling of remorse . . . Did I blurt something out? What did I say?

FOOL: You said that you would not shun death.

SIA: No, I will not, and my life depends on it, because I want to live.

FOOL: Then it's now or never, for here comes your brave and handsome fiancé. A man of silence, they say, but a man of action too. We shall see if he deserves his reputation.

SIA (*going up to the* FOOL *and speaking into his ear*): And what does the legend of Wagadu have to say about Mamadi? What should I do?

FOOL: The legend will say what is says no matter what you do. So do whatever you like. That's the important thing.

(MAMADI *enters. He is dressed all in black, with riding boots and a sword in a scabbard at his side.* SIA *spontaneously moves toward him, arms outstretched, then stops and turns away from him with pretended coquetry, an attitude she maintains throughout their scene. During their dialogue the* FOOL *moves into the shadows and stands with his back to them.*)

SIA: What do you want? What are you doing here?

MAMADI: Kaya Maghan and his priests have deceived me. For two years now I've been fighting in the north with my men against the Almoravida. If not for me, Kumbi would have fallen long ago. And now, today, they reward me by taking my fiancée.

SIA: So?

MAMADI: They're traitors! I owe them nothing. They are men devoid of honor. I no longer owe them obedience. I will not permit this sacrifice to take place.

SIA: And you are right to do so, because you haven't been offered my weight in gold—unlike my father.

MAMADI: Their gold means nothing to me . . .

SIA: But you can still find comfort for my loss, Mamadi, for Kaya Maghan, who thinks of everything, will soon marry you to any woman you want. And . . . from what I hear, you're not as indifferent as you pretend to the charming Maya, of the Cissé clan . . . unless you'd rather have Setan Camara, the new budding beauty of the Kumbis—after me, naturally.

MAMADI: You insult my love for you, Sia . . . but never mind . . .

Sia: Ah, here it is at last: love! After betrayal and tainted honor, after the stamping of boots and the clashing of blades . . . But, as you say, never mind.

MAMADI: I said never mind because it's more important now to live. We don't have much time, and we must act quickly.

SIA: So, answer my question: What do you want?

MAMADI: Run away with me, I'll carry you away from the kingdom of the Snake God. Run away with me. There's not much time, Sia, and none to hesitate.

SIA (*pretending to think hard*): Hesitate . . . you mean . . . between being in the belly of the Snake God or . . . pressed against yours? It's not an easy choice, is it? I'm thinking about the difference, Mamadi . . .

MAMADI: Sia, have you lost your mind? Between that . . . you're hesitating between that . . . that snake . . . and me?

SIA: Oh, Mamadi, don't you know that the serpent and women are old friends? He's our closest confidant; he was our first accomplice. Now that he's become a God, women are free to do whatever they please. I'd like just one last opportunity to enjoy certain little forbidden pleasures.

MAMADI: So, you don't love me any more?

SIA: Unfortunately . . . I do.

MAMADI: What do you mean by that?

SIA (*tenderly*): Mamadi, let me tell you a little secret: I'm proud of having been chosen to be sacrificed.

MAMADI: You're proud to die for . . .

SIA: But if I don't die, it means I'm no longer the most beautiful!

MAMADI: What difference does your beauty make . . .

SIA: What? Don't you care about my beauty? Are you taking back all the compliments you used to pay me?

MAMADI: I'm not taking back anything. You're beautiful, beautiful, beautiful! But I'd rather have you alive.

SIA: Oh, thanks for the concern! But if I don't die, the judges of Kaya Maghan's annual Miss Kumbi contest will manage to come up with some flaw in me before sunrise, and you can be sure there are plenty of other candidates for my crown.

MAMADI: A crown of thorns . . .

SIA: Which poses a thorny question, doesn't it? I too have my honor to defend, Mamadi. Can you see Sia Yatabere reigning only one night and then cast aside for someone else in the morning? I can already hear what all the old cats would say . . . "Huh! Of course she was crowned at night, and the daylight revealed all her defects . . ." No, Mamadi! I want to remain the most beautiful, and in the full light of day!

MAMADI: You will be the most beautiful, but somewhere else. Come away before it's too late!

SIA: Me, let Kumbi down? You really don't know me very well at all, Mamadi. I want to enjoy my triumph here, not somewhere else.

MAMADI: The triumph will lead to death, if you stay.

SIA: Oh, death! I'd forgotten *it*. Let's talk about it for a moment, shall we? Isn't it your second love? Isn't it death you brush against, night and day on the cliffs of Awdaghost? Do you think your death is more honorable than the one that awaits me tonight?

MAMADI: Yes. More honorable because it's more useful to Wagadu.

SIA: But I too am to die so that Wagadu may live.

MAMADI: No one need die for the sake of some priestly mumbo-jumbo. Yes, mumbo-jumbo—which only serves to buttress the faith of the enemies of Wagadu.

SIA: I'm glad to hear you say that. But if you save me from that mumbo-jumbo, as you call it, the death of the other virgin sacrificed in my stead . . . for mumbo-jumbo will still weigh on my mind. Beautiful virgins are like the seven heads of the Wagadu-Bida—as soon as one is struck off, another springs up in its place. So, my brave warrior, perhaps the only weapon is flight after all.

MAMADI (*drawing his sword*): Now I know what I must do!

FOOL (*bursting into laughter*): You should have lived up to your reputation, Mamadi: few words and a lot of action. But I see that your sword is ahead of you.

MAMADI: Who is this man who dares insult me? (*He turns threateningly to the* FOOL).

SIA (*intervening*): It's Kerfa the Fool. He's just saying what he thinks, and whatever he thinks is true.

MAMADI: I would have slain you for your words were you not in the house of the Yatabere.

FOOL: Ha! Ha! Ha! You're too late. My life now belongs to Kaya Maghan and his priests. And, after all, it's more honor to you if I die at their hands, since I've—well, I've only got one head. And even that one's not all it should be . . . Ha ha ha!

SIA (*as* MAMADI *leaves*): This man I love is stupidity itself.

FOOL: No worse that any other real-life hero.

SIA: Do you think he understood what I was trying to say?

FOOL: What difference does it make? The important thing is that his sword understood. He'll act, and think later.

SIA: But what do you think will happen afterwards?

FOOL: You're the only one who will know that.

SIA: What about you? As a matter of fact, what happens to you in the story, Kerfa? You haven't told me what the famous Wagadu legend has to say about you.

FOOL: Ha ha ha! my dear Sia. Every tale has its fool, and he often turns out not to be the character you think. Just remember one thing: fools have no stories. Ha ha! Come, let's go. My time has come, and maybe this evening they'll finally listen to me.

SIA: And don't forget . . .

FOOL: I won't forget, I'll be at the cavern of the Snake God at dawn. Ha! Ha! Ha!

SIA (*as the* FOOL *exits*): Oh . . . I wanted to tell you that tomorrow your meal will be waiting . . . a warm one.

(*The* Fool *exits. It gradually grows dark. The barking and howling of the dogs grows to a crescendo.*)

Fool (*offstage*): Hail, people of Kumbi! Hail, city of Kumbi, City of a thousand lights! Hail to your opulence and your poverty, hail to your men and women . . .

Scene 2

Wakhane Sakho or,
The Horse

(WAKHANE SAKHO *is alone on the stage, he paces back and forth, occasionally glancing toward the entrance. He tries to control his impatience.* MAMADI *the Silent appears.*)

WAKHANE SAKHO: Ah, here you are at last! I've been expecting your visit. My spies told me you were in Kumbi. You realize you're disobeying Kaya Maghan? You are forbidden to see Sia. You must stop at once. Who told you?

MAMADI: Who told me? But didn't you, Uncle? A messenger arrived at a gallop saying you had sent him. He told me that Sia had been chosen for the sacrifice and then rode off again. I set forth at once, and here I am.

WAKHANE SAKHO: I didn't send anyone. I must admit I intended to, but Kaya Maghan and his priests stopped me. You were not to be informed until after the sacrifice.

MAMADI: The traitors! Informed only after the sacrifice! So who sent that man?

WAKHANE SAKHO (*with concern*): I wonder too . . . My men are watching the entire town. No one can enter or leave without my knowledge . . . Unless . . . of course, why didn't I think of it—he's the only one who can come and go as he likes. My men stopped paying attention to him long ago . . . Ha ha ha! Kaya Maghan has really been had! And yet I warned him that the man is dangerous . . .

MAMADI: In any case, he's a brave man.

WAKHANE SAKHO: He's more than brave—he's actually a fool. Kerfa the Fool. Do you know him?

MAMADI: Kerfa the Fool? I met him at Sia's a little while ago. I thought I'd heard his voice somewhere before. He turned his back on me.

WAKHANE SAKHO: That's sure to have been him. He's Sia's protector—or her protegé, who knows. He wanted to do something to help her, and she may have sent him.

MAMADI: I didn't get the impression that he wanted to help her. He hates me and insulted me in the house of the Yatabere. Sia seemed to go along with everything he said. I wanted to escape from Wagadu with her. She wouldn't come with me, and I'm certain that he's the one who urged her to refuse.

WAKHANE SAKHO: It all gets more and more mysterious. But since Sia has refused to go with you, you must now return to the front.

MAMADI: I will not leave. I shall stay in Kumbi.

WAKHANE SAKHO: Listen to me, you romantic fool: you've disobeyed Kaya Maghan by coming here and you are well aware what that means. And I won't go along with you because no one will be able to convince him that I had nothing to do with your being here. And I've no wish to die. (*He gestures to prevent* MAMADI *from interrupting.*) Hear me well: I am the only one who can tell him of your presence here. I will not do so. You will leave the city at once—without being seen, without being recognized. As for my spies who may have seen you enter or leave, they will not speak tomorrow. So go!

MAMADI: Uncle, I will not go.

WAKHANE SAKHO: Well then, you sentimental imbecile, I'll have to get really angry. The girl doesn't want anything more to do with you.

MAMADI: She loves me. She told me so. She never lies.

WAKHANE SAKHO: Very well then, let's admit that she loves you, but she doesn't want to run away with you. She'd rather be sacrificed. And at dawn, she will be. Tomorrow, all of Kumbi will know that you were in my house and that you saw her before the sacrifice. If you want to commit suicide over Sia, well and good, but do it somewhere else, because I have no wish to die.

MAMADI: Uncle, I have made up my mind to kill the Wagadu-Bida.

WAKHANE SAKHO: What are you talking about? I can't believe my ears. Repeat what you just said.

Mamadi: You heard me. I've made up my mind to kill the Wagadu-Bida to save Sia.

Wakhane Sakho (*enunciating very clearly*): You have made up your mind to kill the Snake God of Wagadu . . . Kill the Snake God? And you tell that to *me*, the head of the army and chief of Kaya Maghan's police?

Mamadi: Because I know you will take it like an uncle, not like a head of the army and chief of police.

Wakhane Sakho: Ha ha! It's unbelievable, really unbelievable! Ha ha! That's the second time today someone's said that to me. And do you know who the first one was? Kaya Maghan himself. "Wakhane Sakho has spoken more as the uncle of Mamadi the Silent than as the Leader of my armies and my police." Ha ha ha! I must be getting senile, because that's no compliment to an old warrior like me!

Mamadi: That's not what I meant, Uncle.

Wakhane Sakho: Forget it, my dear nephew . . . or rather, let's not: it makes me proud. It proves that I've still got some heart left, and not just to pump blood. Do you know how I wanted to answer Kaya Maghan? I wanted to say that when the time came I'd remember his words. Thank you, Mamadi.

Mamadi: Why do you thank me, Uncle? I said I had decided to kill the . . .

WAKHANE SAKHO: I thank you for giving me a chance at last to listen to my heart. I've looked forward to this day for eighteen years. Eighteen years, to the day, since my own daughter (*stifling a sob*) was sacrificed to the Wagadu-Bida. Sacrificed in the flower of her youth, like Sia is today. And on that day I didn't even have the courage to act as a father, bound as I was by the grandeur of my name, my blood, my honor. Ah! a coward, that's what I was, just like that fool Yatabere who's strutting with pride today like a barnyard rooster, her own father, as if he were losing just a drop of his *own* blood! Ha! In Wagadu there's a word for illegitimate children—there should be one for illegitimate fathers too—like me . . .

MAMADI: Uncle . . .

WAKHANE SAKHO (*stopping him with a gesture*): No, let me speak. I don't deserve pity. Do you remember her? No, you were only a child . . . We called her "Little Mother" because of how loving she was, because of the way she liked to care for her younger brothers and sisters, and for me too, after the death of your aunt. A girl like no other before her . . .

Little Mother had just passed her eighteenth winter. And on that day—I will never forget the look in her eyes, Mamadi. Her eyes like an antelope cornered by a blood-thirsty pack of dogs. And I, her father—what a father! A wolf among wolves, thirsting for blood, for fame, for honors! Oh, the folly of this world . . . And Little Mother only stared with her huge antelope's eyes . . . And do you know what she said to

156

me? (*He weeps, pushing away* MAMADI, who moves to him.)

In her little girl's voice, she said: Father, blindfold me . . . Father, forgive me, but it's not death I'm afraid of—you've always told me that death is invisible, didn't you? It's the snake . . . the sight of the snake has always made me tremble. Father, take this scarf you brought me from Awdaghost, take it and tie it over my eyes. Please. I'm afraid of snakes, Father. Please, Father, use that scarf, it's mine . . .

And do you know, Mamadi, what I did that day? Do you know? (*He cries out.*) I refused to do it! Yes, I refused! Refused! And why? For honor and all its stupid cohorts! So that no one would say that a daughter of my blood had been afraid to look death in the face. (*weeping again*) And Little Mother's huge eyes, still pleading with me . . . and her little girl's body, already beginning to tremble . . . (*He falls to his knees in tears.*) And they forgot . . . they told me that they forgot . . . all those who say that memory is the world's root—they all forgot Little Mother.

MAMADI (*helping him to rise*): Come, Uncle, get up. For Little Mother and for Sia, I must go to rid us all forever of this monster.

WAKHANE SAKHO: Wait, Mamadi, it's not yet time. He won't leave his cavern until dawn. Before that, they will go with Sia to thank the twelve founding clans and then to the tomb of Din'ga the Ancestor to ask forgiveness for the living. When you hear the drums of Din'ga beat for the third time, that will be the

157

moment. In the meantime, hear me for I have something very important to tell you.

MAMADI: Speak, Uncle, and I will obey you.

WAKHANE SAKHO: This will be the last time you will obey anyone, for tomorrow you will be Kaya Maghan!

MAMADI: I, Kaya Maghan! But that's impossible, Uncle.

WAKHANE SAKHO: Indispensable, my nephew! And don't bring up loyalty to the crown. You have broken the Pact and betrayed Kaya Maghan. There isn't room enough for both of you.

MAMADI: I betrayed no one! They're the traitors.

WAKHANE SAKHO: Ha ha ha! Listen to me, you fool! Eighteen years ago, I was a coward with Little Mother, and I've been a coward ever since with Kaya Maghan. That is my only reason for living, my revenge against myself. The day after Little Mother was sacrificed, Kaya Maghan made me head of his armies and his police. Probably to console me for my daughter's loss. But what he doesn't know is that for eighteen years I've worked against him . . .

MAMADI: You, Uncle!

WAKHANE SAKHO: Yes, me, Wakhane Sakho! For eighteen years I've conspired against the crown. I've been plotting in the shadows. Slowly, I've put out invisible tentacles over all of Wagadu. I've alienated the people from Kaya Maghan by hunting down and torturing and murdering innocent people, all in his name. I've forced those who were against him to dance to his tune. Islam has spread into his very palace, and I have let it happen, I've even encouraged it—not out of faith, but out of hatred, to bring about his fall, by whatever means! I have even had a hand in creating Kerfa himself. For eighteen years I've been controlling the shadows by making a false light of day shine around Kaya Maghan . . . But now we're coming to the end. My end, perhaps, for they are beginning to suspect something. More than once, I've had the feeling I was being toyed with . . . during the priests' council, even by Kaya Maghan himself. We must act quickly now, my nephew, for in politics there is no such thing as loyal combat, as there is on the battlefield. At the slightest scratch, you play dead and conceal your weapon. Let your adversary walk past you and then, when his back is turned, get up quickly and strike!

MAMADI: I shall strike at the Wagadu-Bida, Uncle, but do you really think that the people will make me Kaya Maghan for that?

WAKHANE SAKHO: No! The people will turn against you as long as Kaya Maghan and his priests lead them. They will pursue you to Bambuk if they have to, they will put you to death. The people will dance on your body, because they only back the man who holds the whip.

MAMADI: So I must kill Kaya Maghan and his priests?

WAKHANE SAKHO: Never! Then they would die sinless! The man who must die is the only truly pure man in Kumbi.

MAMADI: And who is this man, if he exists?

WAKHANE SAKHO: Kerfa the Fool.

MAMADI: But if he's innocent . . .

WAKHANE SAKHO: All the more reason to kill him.

MAMADI: I thought Kaya Maghan and his priests were going to do that.

WAKHANE SAKHO: It's not as simple as I thought. I wanted Kerfa the Fool dead, and I had planned it all very carefully. In politics you can't afford to make mistakes, and Kaya Maghan is clever. He knows that Kerfa the Fool is the most popular man in Kumbi, the man most heeded by the people. He spoke to him. I tried to dissuade him, but he sent me packing. However, confidential sources have informed me that he tried to get Kerfa to come over to his side, against us.

MAMADI: You must really have spies everywhere!

WAKHANE SAKHO: Even in Kaya Maghan's bed, and since there are so many of them, I defy anyone to uncover them! If he had succeeded in forging an alliance with Kerfa, I would now be a hunted man. But Kerfa the Fool has no friends. He despises everyone, and even Sia is nothing but the tool of his madness.

After their meeting, Kaya Maghan summoned us, the three priests of the Sacred Forest and me. It was decided that Kerfa the Fool must have his tongue cut out.

MAMADI: His tongue cut— But why? It would have been simpler just to have him killed!

WAKHANE SAKHO: Ha! Ha! What a fool you are! You are good at fighting, but your political education is sadly deficient. I will see to that. Kerfa is more dangerous dead than alive. But he must be silenced, for his words make the people think, and a people who think . . . If Kerfa is murdered, he will become a martyr, and there's nothing like a martyr to inspire an uprising among the people. Alive, they will go on listening to him, but dead, his words will be translated into deeds. If we silence him by cutting out his tongue, the people will have no more guide. And you know what happens to those who are suddenly blinded . . . If reason is to prevail, fools must be silenced.

MAMADI: Do you think people will stand idly by when they learn that Kaya Maghan has had the tongue of Kerfa the Fool cut out?

WAKHANE SAKHO: Who will tell them? Not Kerfa the Fool—he won't be able to speak. The people will never know the truth. You see, Nephew, people like mysteries, the whole art of governing rests upon that fact. Tomorrow, reason will tell them that Kerfa was subjected to the punishment of the Primal Word, that it deprived him of the power of the borrowed word because he had blasphemed. And only Kaya Maghan, myself and the priests of the Sacred Forest will share the secret of the gods.

MAMADI: Let me get this straight, Uncle: you will have Kerfa killed and see that Kaya Maghan and his priests are blamed for it. Kerfa will become a martyr, unrest will grow, the people will rise up against Kaya Maghan.

WAKHANE SAKHO: With the help of my concealed agents . . .

MAMADI: And I will kill the Wagadu-Bida, save Sia, and the people will hail me as a hero and a liberator.

WAKHANE SAKHO: And we will lead them off to the green plains of Bambuk.

MAMADI: But why leave, since we will be the masters?

WAKHANE SAKHO: Because all must be accomplished. Kumbi must be razed to the last stone, and the Sacred Forest must be burned to the ground.

MAMADI: You will destroy Kumbi, Uncle?

WAKHANE SAKHO: The Almoravida will do that. I will withdraw the troops from the northern front, evacuate the city's inhabitants and open wide the gates.

MAMADI: You're mad, Uncle! I can never allow you to do that . . . After all, I am a warrior.

WAKHANE SAKHO: If you refuse, I shall have you arrested at once, and Sia will die at dawn, as planned. If you agree, you know my conditions. Take it or leave it.

MAMADI: But why . . . Why would you want Kumbi destroyed?

WAKHANE SAKHO: When one kills the gods, the world must be remade. Kumbi and the world of Din'ga, the world of the Wagadu-Bida, the world of the hyena and the vulture. A world steeped in the blood of the innocent, crushed beneath its luxuries, its gold and its palaces. I sound just like Kerfa. And he's right. All that must die away, and Kerfa too, so that a new world can be born. And we will move to the plains of Bambuk to create it. We will all set out together, marching day and night if need be.

MAMADI: Uncle, we'll march in vain, for the eyes of Little Mother will follow you, wherever we go . . .

WAKHANE SAKHO (*in terror*): No! Never say that again! Never! Do you understand?

MAMADI: They will follow you.

WAKHANE SAKHO: Silence! Be silent! We will leave, we will walk, we will go even farther than Bambuk if we must. (*There is a roll of drums; he puts his hand on his sword.*) So what is your decision? Speak! (*A long pause. There is another roll of drums.*)

MAMADI: Agreed. We will walk, and if the green plains of Bambuk do not exist, I will invent them for Sia.

WAKHANE SAKHO: Those who enter the Sacred Forest never emerge again. Take my horse and it will guide you. He knows the way. See that the point of your spear is sharp, and you don't forget that the Wagadu-Bida has seven heads.

MAMADI: Sia told me that—why seven heads, Uncle?

WAKHANE SAKHO (*teasing*): Do you know the seven deadly sins, ninny?

MAMADI: No, Uncle, not yet.

WAKHANE SAKHO: Well, Sia will teach you about them, ninny.

MAMADI: Because this isn't politics any longer? Is that it, uncle?

WAKHANE SAKHO: No, not at all. Politics is the eighth deadly sin. You've already tasted that one, and now may you enjoy it.

(*A third roll of drums.* MAMADI *exits. Blackout.*)

ACT III

SCENE 1

THE PAWNS

Day. The masked chorus; the CHIEF, *the* ASSISTANT CHIEF *and the* FLUNKY *stand to one side, next to the entrance. The* SHACKLED CHORUS, *the* BLIND CHORUS *and the* MUTE CHORUS, *gagged, stand apart from them.*)

CHIEF: The curtain is going up, let us announce that we are about to begin.

ASSISTANT CHIEF: It's daybreak here—and elsewhere too perhaps. Let us announce the good bad news.

FLUNKY: We were expecting water—and instead we got fire!

CHIEF: Rumors are beginning to spread.

ASSISTANT CHIEF: They are spreading through the bush. The bush is dry. The fire is beginning to gather strength and spread. The bush is burning.

CHIEF: Rumors are beginning to spread.

ASSISTANT CHIEF: The farms are beginning to burn. The fire is drawing nearer. It has reached the main street.

CHIEF: Rumors are beginning to spread.

FLUNKY: The flames are spreading. Ah! They are licking at the palace walls.

CHIEF: And rumors are beginning to spread. Have you heard the rumors, my brothers? Kerfa the Fool died last night.

BLIND CHORUS: We didn't see anything, but we heard all about it. Kerfa was murdered. May his murderers be accursed!

CHIEF: We saw and we heard. Kerfa the Fool was murdered by Kaya Maghan and his priests.

SHACKLED CHORUS: Accursed be the murderers of Kerfa!

CHIEF (*aside*): His remains are beginning to burn. Let us quench the flames.

(*The* MASKED CHORUS *mimes discovering* KERFA's *imaginary body.*)

ASSISTANT CHIEF: Behold the body of Kerfa the Fool, or what's left of it.

FLUNKY: The body of Kerfa the Fool is covered in blood.

CHIEF: They've put out his eyes.

BLIND CHORUS: We will be his eyes and see for him.

THE LEGEND OF WAGADU AS SEEN BY SIA YATABERE

ASSISTANT CHIEF: They've broken his legs.

SHACKLED CHORUS: We will be his legs and walk for him.

FLUNKY: They've cut out his tongue.

SHACKLED CHORUS and BLIND CHORUS: We will be his tongue and cry out for him. Death to Kaya Maghan and to his priests!

CHIEF: Kerfa dared insult the Kaya Maghan.

SHACKLED CHORUS: Death to Kaya Maghan, who put us in chains!

ASSISTANT CHIEF: Kerfa dared to insult the priests of the Sacred Forest.

BLIND CHORUS: Death to the priests of the Sacred Forest, who put out our eyes.

FLUNKY: Kerfa dared to insult the Snake God of Wagadu.

MUTE CHORUS: Death to the Snake God of Wagadu, who gagged us!

(*The* FLUNKY *dashes to the* MUTE CHORUS *and puts back the gag. They begin to weep.*)

CHIEF (*aside*): Perfect. The fire is spreading nicely. Let us now attack the big game.

ASSISTANT CHIEF: The rumor is spreading. Have you heard the rumor, my brothers? Everyone is saying that the Snake God of Wagadu has been killed.

FLUNKY: Wagadu-Bida is dead, slain by Mamadi the Silent.

BLIND CHORUS: Hail Mamadi the Silent, avenger of Kerfa's blood.

CHIEF: The Mute Chorus has stopped weeping. Look at their eyes . . . they're smiling.

BLIND CHORUS: We cannot see it, but we can sense it. The Mute Chorus can smile again. Mamadi the Silent is a hero.

SHACKLED CHORUS: We cannot feel it, but we can see it. The Mute Chorus can smile again. Mamadi the Silent is our savior.

CHIEF: Wagadu-Bida is dead. Kaya Maghan has betrayed his people and the priests have been stripped of their power. We are now orphans. What is to become of us?

BLIND CHORUS: We have Mamadi the Silent, our beloved hero.

FLUNKY: And who will be our Kaya Maghan?

SHACKLED CHORUS: Mamadi the Silent will be our new Kaya Maghan.

CHORUSES (*together*): Kaya Maghan is dead! Long live Kaya Maghan!

CHIEF (*aside*): It's like a furnace, now. (*rubbing his hands*) And now we come to the hardest part—the master's voice.

ASSISTANT CHIEF: The rumor is spreading . . . have you heard the rumor, my brothers?

FLUNKY: Mamadi slew the Wagadu Bida while mounted on the horse of Wakhane Sakho.

BLIND CHORUS: Long live the steed of Wakhane Sakho!

CHIEF (*aside*): That didn't work. Let's try something else. Try going for the emotions.

ASSISTANT CHIEF: Wakhane Sakho is the beloved uncle of Mamadi the Silent!

SHACKLED CHORUS: Long live the beloved nephew of Wakhane Sakho!

CHIEF: Darn! That didn't work either! The Master doesn't seem to help feed the flames at all.

FLUNKY: You must admit, he was probably too much a part of the former regime! Would you like me to give it a try, Chief?

CHIEF: No thank you! You'd get him hanged on the spot. Let him look after himself. We've done what's essential. We can be glad they're not calling for his head. Right now, we'd better pay attention to the fire.

MUTE CHORUS and SHACKLED CHORUS (*walking around the* MASKED CHORUS): We want—to see—our hero! We want—to see—our new Kaya Maghan!

CHIEF: It's time. Give the signal, Flunky.

(*The* FLUNKY *beats the drum. Mamadi and Wakhane Sakho enter.*)

CHIEF: Behold—

FLUNKY (*interrupting the* CHIEF, *who looks at him furiously*): Behold the hero of the day! A nobody at sunrise, Kaya Maghan at noon! With him is his beloved uncle, Wakhane Sakho, whose brave steed did not shrink from confronting the spirits of the Sacred Forest. Long live nephew and uncle!

CHIEF: You could have waited your turn and not tried to hog all the glory!

BLIND CHORUS and SHACKLED CHORUS: Long live our new Kaya Maghan! Honor to the nephew, honor to the uncle's steed!

FLUNKY (*aside*): We should do it again and seize the advantage, for if this works my promotion is a sure thing . . . I'll be leader of the Masked Chorus, instead of that big dope there. (*He moves behind the* MUTE CHORUS *and begins to egg them on.*) Honor to Wakhane

Sakho! Repeat after me: Honor to the uncle! (*realizing his error*) Darn! wrong chorus—trust me to pick the one that can't talk! (*He sheepishly returns to his place.*)

MAMADI (*to* WAKHANE SAKHO): The gold on your armor is tarnished, uncle. Memories are hard to wipe away.

WAKHANE SAKHO: Don't worry about me, and don't mention gold. I am now your major domo and adviser. Leave things to me. (*addressing the* CHORUSES) People of Wagadu! The Snake God is dead, and all things are now possible.

SHACKLED CHORUS: Since all things are possible, free us from our chains! And we will dance the *worosso* with our hero.

BLIND CHORUS: Give us back our sight, and we will dance the *worosso* with our new Kaya Maghan.

(WAKHANE SAKHO *goes to the* CHORUSES *to free them*)

FLUNKY (*aside*): Let's make a bet: if he frees them, it's his grave they'll dance on.

WAKHANE SAKHO: Just a minute. (*He hesitates and then stops.*) Hear me: you will all be freed. Are you not free already? But we must begin at the beginning. Do not forget, I am the major domo, the master of ceremonies and therefore the master of order! We must first immortalize the great words of our great philosopher, Kerfa the Fool.

171

CHORUSES (*together*): We will honor the great words of
Kerfa the Fool. We will do even more than that! But
first, free us! Free us first! Free us first!

WAKHANE SAKHO: Order! I must have order first! Let
us hear the great words of Kerfa the Fool as he was so
basely interrupted by Kaya Maghan and his priests.
(*aside*) What was he saying . . . Oh, yes, I've got it!
(*To the* CHORUSES, *in the tones of a public storyteller*)
When the night was drawing to a close, the priests of
the Sacred Forest came to seek Sia Yatabere and
escort her to the cavern of the Snake God. In the
meantime, Mamadi the Silent had gone to Wakhane
Sakho, his uncle, who was chief of the armies and
chief of the police of Kaya Maghan, and he said unto
him: "My uncle, I will kill the Wagadu Bida to save Sia
from death. You must chose between heart and
mind." And Wakhane Sakho replied unto him: "Mamadi, I could have arrested you on the spot and
turned you over to the justice of Kaya Maghan, his
priests and his false god, but both the voice of the
heart and the voice of the mind tell me that we must
save all the people of Wagadu. Go then, slay the
monster, and afterwards do us the honor of being our
Kaya Maghan. I would go with you, were my arms not
too old, but take my horse. He will guide you through
the labyrinth of the Sacred Forest. And don't forget:
the Wagadu Bida has seven heads."

BLIND CHORUS: Honor to Wakhane Sakho!

CHIEF: Oof! He finally managed to get through that all
right! But that stupid Blind Chorus will probably
manage to see through us.

WAKHANE SAKHO: Mamadi the Silent, our new Kaya Maghan, will continue the great words. Henceforth, he is their master and protector.

MAMADI: Once at the monster's cave, I hid myself in the underbrush until the time was ripe. Sia stood before the cavern, beautiful and motionless, like a statue of ebony. At last the monster appeared. I flung myself upon it: the battle was a fearsome one. The moon herself hid behind the treetops, the sun dared not rise, and the clouds fled from the sky, which began to turn red from the blood that gushed up to it. With one final blow of my sword I cut off the monster's seventh head, which flew into the air with an awful curse: It cried out: "For seven years, for seven months and for seven days no drop of water will fall upon Wagadu, and your gold will turn to sand."

(He falls silent. A long silence. The CHORUSES *look at each other and seem to be unsure how to take the news.)*

WAKHANE SAKHO: What difference does that make? We will set out for the green plains of Bambuk, where there is water in abundance, and we will have the gold of the Bouré beneath our feet.

SHACKLED CHORUS: To the green plains of Bambuk— but first, free us from our chains! (WAKHANE SAKHO *removes their chains.*)

BLIND CHORUS: Give us back our sight and we will dance the *worosso* all the way to the green plains of

Bambuk. (WAKHANE Sakho *removes the blindfold from their eyes.*)

CHIEF (*to the other members of the* MASKED CHORUS): We will stay as we are, for anonymity is the best companion of freedom.

WAKHANE SAKHO: Now, people of Wagadu, let us dance the *worosso* with Mamadi the Silent all the way to the green plains of Bambuk.

(*The* FLUNKY *beats the drum.* WAKHANE SAKHO *notices the* MUTE CHORUS.)

WAKHANE SAKHO: What about you—why aren't you singing?

CHIEF: Master, can't you see that they have not yet been freed?

WAKHANE SAKHO: I grant them their freedom now. Let them sing!

FLUNKY: I'll be damned if anyone can sing with their mouth gagged!

WAKHANE SAKHO: Oh, yes—I forgot. (*He goes to the* MUTE CHORUS *and removes the gag.*) You could have asked me, like the others. They always have to be different, don't they? Now, let's be serious: drums!

(*The* FLUNKY *starts to beat the drum and then stops.*)

THE LEGEND OF WAGADU AS SEEN BY SIA YATABERE

FLUNKY: Master, they're still not singing.

WAKHANE SAKHO: What do you want now? You asked for speech and you have it. What more do you want? Do I still frighten you? Well, Flunky . . . you ask them what they want.

FLUNKY (*approaching the* MUTE CHORUS): Master, they say that they won't sing until they've seen Sia Yatabere . . .

MAMADI: Sia? Oh yes . . . You know women, uncle . . . how they like ceremonies. She's making herself beautiful before showing herself to her subjects.

SIA (*She appears wearing a white dress that is wrinkled and bloodstained.*): I don't need to make myself beautiful, Mamadi. I've always been so, and I always will be. But you're forgetting that Kerfa the Fool loathed your songs and dances. Let the drums be silent, and then we will speak.

MAMADI: We've already said everything. There's nothing more to say.

SIA: Even Wakhane Sakho?

WAKHANE SAKHO (*to* MAMADI): What's going on? What are you two up to? (*to* SIA): Why are you looking at me like that, Sia? Your eyes . . . Why do your eyes . . . Is it really you? Don't come any closer! (*He trembles.*)

175

SIA: Sia's body—with Little Mother's Eyes. You tremble now, horseman, but you will tremble even more when you know the truth.

WAKHANE SAKHO: The truth? What truth? What are you hiding from me? Mamadi, I must know.

MAMADI: There's nothing to say, I tell you; everything has been said. The girl has gone mad.

SIA: Then I will speak.

MAMADI: No, wait. *I* will speak. Master of ceremonies, have the people withdraw.

WAKHANE SAKHO: Did you hear? Your Kaya Maghan asks you to withdraw. Our meeting will be private, and I will give you a detailed report later. Go! This is how things are done in courts all over the world. (*The* CHORUSES *exit*) We are alone. I am listening.

MAMADI: Wakhane Sakho, you're the master of ceremonies. Announce the play.

Scene 2

WAGADU BIDA

(SIA, WAKHANE SAKHO, MAMADI *the Silent. The stage is dark. There are three drumrolls.*)

WAKHANE SAKHO (*offstage*): Let the play begin! Behold the sacrificial day, the twilight of the virgins of Kumbi. Mamadi the Silent alights from his horse. He advances, sword in hand, to the monster's cave. (*Light comes up on* MAMADI *the Silent*) In the sky, a curtain of clouds, revealing Sia Yatabere. (*Light comes up on* SIA.)

MAMADI: Sia, there you are at last. I thought I would never find you.

SIA: What do you want? Who are you?

MAMADI: Sia, it's me, Mamadi. I've come to slay the monster.

SIA: Kerfa the Fool is the one I want to see. Go find him.

MAMADI: Kerfa the Fool can't come. There's not much time. The monster will soon emerge from his cave. Move out of the way so that I can strike him.

SIA: I won't move until I've seen Kerfa the Fool. He promised me he'd be here at dawn.

MAMADI: Be reasonable, Sia. Move out of the way, unless you want to die. There's not much time, and Kerfa will not be coming.

177

SIA: Then go! I'll stay here and await my death.

MAMADI: But Sia, not long ago you wanted to live. I will slay the monster for you.

SIA: I've changed my mind now. I'd rather die . . . unless you find Kerfa the Fool.

MAMADI: I'd never have time to go look for him in Kumbi and come back here to kill the monster. You'd be dead by then. Listen to me, for God's sake! Let me kill him first, and then I'll find Kerfa the Fool for you.

SIA: It's now or never! Go find him, Mamadi, I want to tell him something.

MAMADI: You haven't got anything to tell him because he won't be coming. Kerfa is dead, Sia—do you hear? He's been murdered by Kaya Maghan and his priests.

SIA: You're lying, Mamadi—you know as well as I do that no blood but mine is to be spilled on the day of the sacrifice. Kerfa is to die tomorrow, not today.

MAMADI: I swear to you on my honor that Kerfa has been murdered.

SIA: Murdered by you! You hated him. I was there when you threatened to kill him . . .

MAMADI: I didn't kill Kerfa, I swear it . . .

SIA: On your honor as a murderer and a liar. If Kaya
Maghan and his priests had killed him, you would
have told me right away, because you hate them too.
Out of my sight, murderer! I'd rather die a thousand
deaths than live at your hand. Out of my sight,
murderer!

MAMADI: Sia, don't talk like that! It wasn't me, I swear it!
Let me slay the beast, and then I'll tell you who killed
Kerfa.

WAKHANE SAKHO (*offstage*): Tenderhearted fool! And
just when I had everything all planned. But the girl is
a lot more intelligent than I thought . . .

SIA (*putting on a seductive air*): Mamadi, my love, my lion
of the cliffs of Awdaghost . . . I want to live, I want
to live with you, I will be your slave if you wish . . . I
hear the monster stirring behind me. I want to live,
but if you don't tell me the murderer's name, I'll
throw myself into the cave!

MAMADI: No! Sia, don't! It was my uncle, Wakhane
Sakho, who had Kerfa the Fool murdered.

SIA: You're still lying to me, Mamadi. Wakhane Sakho is
only the arm of Kaya Maghan. And Kaya Maghan
would not have had Kerfa killed today. Farewell.

(*She moves to throw herself into the Wagadu Bida's cave.*)

MAMADI: No, wait! Wakhane Sakho was not acting on
Kaya Maghan's orders. He was acting alone.

SIA: How do you know? Wakhane Sakho is not the kind of man who shares his plans, not even with his own son. Unless you were in it together.

MAMADI: Sia, listen to me. You have to understand that we were acting in your interests, in the interests of Wagadu. It's not enough just to slay the monster. Kaya Maghan and his priests would then have killed us all. Wakhane Sakho thought that we must arouse the wrath of the people against the crown and win them over by killing Kerfa the Fool and making them believe that he had been killed at Kaya Maghan's orders. Something had to be done, and I wouldn't have been able to save you from death because he would have had me arrested. Now you know everything. So stand aside and let me carry out our plan.

SIA: Yes—that's it, carry out your plan. First Kerfa, then the monster and finally the throne of Kaya Maghan. Wipe everything out and start all over again . . .

MAMADI: We'll discuss it later, Sia. Right now, stand aside, because I must slay the monster before it's too late.

SIA (*casually*): Don't trouble yourself. There is no monster.

MAMADI: What do you mean? Have you gone mad? Stand aside, Sia.

SIA: I said: the Wagadu Bida doesn't exist. It never existed outside our imagination.

MAMADI: I don't understand . . . or maybe I'm the one who's going mad. Then why do the priests of the Sacred Forest . . . Kaya Maghan . . . and all those virgins sacrificed . . .

SIA: It's been one long masquerade from the beginning. Just one big trick—and we were all taken in by it. Except for Kaya Maghan and his priests, of course—they were running the whole thing.

MAMADI: But if there wasn't a Wagadu Bida, what did they do with all the virgins?

SIA: Their bleached bones are lying down there at the bottom of this well that is supposed to be the cave of the Snake God.

MAMADI: But why all this charade?

SIA: Kerfa the Fool may have known why . . . But if he knew, why did he let me descend into this hell? I remember his words: "The one with the softest fleece, the tenderest flesh, the soft, thick wool quivering at the man's touch. The blade caresses her slowly before it makes its sudden slash. Her back stiffens, she struggles to free herself from his tight embrace, her eyes roll up, she goes into a final spasm and then her last gasp . . . And then death. Pleasure or pain—what does it matter? To die while the blood of her lost virginity still flows . . ." I remember Kerfa's long hoarse cry before he fell sobbing at my feet. That cry that I heard seven times—do you hear, Mamadi?—seven times before dawn, in my arms.

MAMADI: Sia! What are you talking about?

SIA: You won't understand Kerfa's words either—his cry. Ah! Seven times I was taken, Mamadi, seven times I was raped, and at each cry my virgin blood . . .

MAMADI (*trembling*): Sia, who did this?

SIA: Ah, now you're trembling, Mamadi. As if that were more horrible than all the Snake Gods, right? Who but your seven priests of the Sacred Forest, who pretend to have abandoned all worldly things. Ah! You sow, they reap, after they've chosen the best seed. And how many virgins to perish for the Wagadu—happy, sad, but always proud—have been humiliated here in their deepest being, in their souls, how many have fled down this path and been caught and killed in the traps set for them in this forest where no one gets out alive? How many have then thrown themselves headlong into the well for shame? But I, Sia Yatabere, I said no to death. I slaked my thirst with my virgin blood, it filled my entire body and I vomited it out, I spat it to the sky that it might fall down like a rain of blood on your green plains of Bambuk.

Seven times, for seven years I cursed the water and the gold of the Wagadu, to the seventh day of the seventh month.

(*She rises and moves to the wings as the stage grows completely dark.*)

A curse upon you and your uncle, Mamadi. May the innocent blood that has been spilled be upon your heads! Sing! Dance! But know that I alone am the keeper of Kerfa's word. Know that the Fool has no history. Nor does woman. I will witness yours.

(*The light comes up again.* MAMADI *is standing with* WAKHANE SAKHO.)

MAMADI: You can guess what happened next. I killed the priests, I led Sia out of the Sacred Forest and then set fire to it. The fire spread to the old city and then to the palace. At this very moment Kaya Maghan and his last remaining followers are living through Kumbi's final hour.

WAKHANE SAKHO: Why did you lie and say you had slain the Snake God?

MAMADI: First, because the people needed a hero. There hasn't been one in this story. And then, you told me that mystery was an art by which one governed. I took the mystery of Kaya Maghan and his priests and became for the people a king who had dethroned a God.

WAKHANE SAKHO: But why didn't you say anything to me?

MAMADI: Hadn't Kaya Maghan and his priests told you that the Wagadu Bida didn't exist?

WAKHANE SAKHO: No, I never knew.

MAMADI: Well, I only followed their example. The State needs continuity, Uncle!

WAKHANE SAKHO: You're right. But I wonder if Kaya Maghan himself knew . . .

MAMADI: And Kerfa the Fool?

WAKHANE SAKHO: We'll never know now. And after all, there has to be some mystery in the story, since it has no hero.

MAMADI: But it does have a victor: Power.

WAKHANE SAKHO: You mustn't believe that, Nephew. Indeed, you must not believe that, for that is what your predecessors believed. You see, no one could have suspected that the day would end as it has . . . Yesterday, you were not Kaya Maghan and today you are, but what do you know about tomorrow? The sun sinks below the horizon and the green plains of Bambuk are still far away . . . My poor Little Mother, who was so afraid of snakes . . .

EPILOGUE

(*The* MASKED CHORUS, *made up of the* CHIEF, *the* ASSISTANT CHIEF, *the* BLIND CHORUS *and the* MUTE CHORUS)

CHIEF: Night falls on the crossroads that lead nowhere. The curtains fall. The spectacle is ending, life goes on.

ASSISTANT CHIEF: The spectacle is life, with all its actors. (*to audience*) Oh, don't worry, they're not the same ones.

CHIEF: Yesterday's masters are not today's.

FLUNKY: And today's will certainly not be tomorrow's.

CHIEF: Mind your tongue, idiot. (*to audience*) The Master has demoted him from Flunky to Assistant Flunky . . . for his "disservices" to the people. *Somebody had to take the blame*. (*to* FLUNKY) And everyone saw how you treated the Blind Chorus—idiot, coward, you dope. So mind your tongue. Assistant Chief!

ASSISTANT CHIEF: Today's people are not yesterday's people.

CHIEF: They exchanged yesterday's rags for today's rags.

FLUNKY: New holiday clothes wear out quickly. They're never worth much.

CHIEF: No personal remarks, Assistant Flunky, or you'll be demoted again! Assistant Chief!

185

ASSISTANT CHIEF: We're the only one's who haven't changed, because we're the Master's noble ears, his breath, his ability. We are the masked chorus, the faceless chorus.

CHIEF (*aside, raising his fist to the* FLUNKY): If he says "the coreless chorus" again this time, I'll get him. I'll rip off his mask and land him one right on the nose!

FLUNKY: You've got to admit, Chief, that wearing a mask is great—the anonymity is very comforting.

CHIEF: Yes, it hides your ugly snout!

FLUNKY: My snout? Where does that big lug get off talking about my snout? Has he seen his own . . .

CHIEF: Quiet, Flunky! And get to work, it's almost time. As for you, Assistant Chief, stand behind the tree and listen to what they say, and you, Flunky, hide behind that pile of garbage and try to find out what they're thinking. And don't forget, you are to report back at dawn. (*They exit on either side while the* SHACKLED CHORUS, BLIND CHORUS *and* MUTE CHORUS *enter, walking slowly in single file.*)

BLIND CHORUS: Onward, onward. Night and day we march; year in, year out, and still we march. Shackled Chorus, you who have eyes to guide you, can you see the green plains of Bambuk?

SHACKLED CHORUS: Brothers, our new chains are heavy ones. We stopped marching long ago, Blind Chorus.

They made us march night and day, year in, year out. And brothers, as far as we can see there is nothing but the unsetting sun that burns into our eyes.

BLIND CHORUS: Can the Mute Chorus see the green plains of Bambuk?

SHACKLED CHAINS: The eyes of the Mute Chorus are filled with tears. We would drink them to quench our thirst, but they are bitter tears.

BLIND CHORUS: Courage, brothers. We will be free as soon as the green plains of Bambuk come into view. Isn't that what they promised us? In the meanwhile, it seems we must continue to be disciplined in all things, we must live by sweat and sacrifice . . .

SHACKLED CHORUS: Don't talk about sacrifice . . . we've had enough of that by now. And you'd have to be blind to believe in their green plains of Bambuk. Happy are those who have no eyes to see. But your ears must be good for something, aren't they, Blind Chorus?

BLIND CHORUS: Who can you believe? They even say that Sia is mad, that she even admits it.

SHACKLED CHORUS: To all intents and purposes it's true, isn't it? Isn't that the first decree they issued after their so-called private conference? (*with emphasis*) Sia Yatabere has been found insane by the members of the Crown Council, made up of Mamadi the Silent, hero of the Sacred Forest, conqueror of the Bida and new Kaya Maghan, his uncle, councilor and master of

187

ceremonies, the brave Wakhane Sakho—they really didn't need to include his noble steed that boldly braved the pitfalls of the Sacred Forest and the Wagadu Bida! Oof! It didn't take that many grand titles and attributes to declare that Kerfa was insane, and he admitted he was a fool. What difference does it make—truth has no age, my brothers, and no name.

BLIND CHORUS: Yes, my brother, you may be right. In any event, when *she* speaks it's as though a ray of light pierces the blackness of eternal night.

SHACKLED CHORUS: I feel that too, my brother: when she speaks, my chains become light as feathers and I dream I am a bird. And have you noticed that even the Mute Chorus stops weeping and begins to smile . . . Oh, excuse me, I keep forgetting you can't see. And it's about time for her arrival. I can hear the dogs barking. She will finally come. We must hide if we want to stay and listen to her, for their spies are everywhere. Let's hide and listen . . . (*They disappear upstage.*)

GLORIA VICTIS!

(*The stage is completely dark. SIA suddenly appears in a circle of light. The barking of the dogs grows louder, drowning out her voice. As she crosses the stage the spotlight blinks on and off, plunging the stage into darkness and, when lighted again, picks out SIA. She is naked. After she has exited, we see nothing but a harsh light on a naked and silent stage.*)

Charlotte-Arrisoa Rafenomanjato, a former midwife and clinic director, began to write after having raised three children. Her plays often deal with the traditions and history of Madagascar. Rafenomanjato's first play, *Le prix de la paix*, won second prize in Radio France Internationale's 1986 Inter-African Theatre Competition. A filmed version was later televised in several countries. Her second play, *La pécheresse*, won fourth prize in 1987. *The Herd* was a finalist in 1990. *Le prince de l'étang* was performed in France at the Limoges Festival and in Italy, where it was published by Bulzoni Editore. She has published two novels, *Le pétale écarlate*, and *Probabilisme*, and a book of poetry. She is active in organizing and aiding the writers of Madagascar.

Marjolijn de Jager was born in Indonesia and educated in the Netherlands and the U.S. She received her doctorate in Romance Languages and Literatures in 1975. She has translated Dutch poetry and prose, including some works of Hugo Claus, and many works by women poets. Since 1986 she has focused on francophone African writers. Her most recent translation is *Before the Birth of the Moon* by V. Y. Mudimbe published by Fireside/Simon & Schuster. Her translation of *The Abandoned Baobab*, the autobiography of the Senegalese woman author Ken Bugul, is published by Lawrence Hill Books.

The premiere of the English translation of *The Herd* was directed in a staged reading by Rodney Scott Hudson at Ubu Repertory Theater on May 1, 1991.

CHARACTERS

FALY, *a dwarf, 26, a peasant and cowherd*
RAKEVA, *Faly's father*
DODA, *Faly's brother*
MAVO, *Faly's sister*
RAVO, *Faly's friend, a teacher*
LALATIANA, *Ravo's fiancée*
RAOZY, *a townswoman, seller of rice cakes*

THE VILLAGE CHIEF
HAGA, *a peasant*
RASOLO, *the guard of a public building*
RANGO, *a peasant woman*
BLIND BEGGAR
WOMAN PLAINTIFF
TWO ROBBERS
TWO PASSERS-BY
POLICE INSPECTOR
POLICE COMMISSIONER
MAN WITH SUITCASES

SCENE 1

(A clearing at dusk; sounds of lowing and stamping of a herd; the cracking of a whip and cries of the cowherd are heard. LALATIANA *is weaving a wicker basket.* RAVO *is playing a* valiha.[1] FALY *enters, skipping and snapping his whip.)*

LALATIANA *(calls out)*: I want to play, I want to skip rope with you! *(She catches up with him. The whip becomes their jump rope.)*

RAVO *(singing with his* valiha): You, children without innocence, could not conquer the years.

LALATIANA *(joyfully)*: Sovereign without a crown, delight is our kingdom.

RAVO: You, dreamers of a pillaged world, your joyfulness blinds you. The sun has drunk the water of the universe, the earth turns into dust . . . like a lifeless body.

FALY *(stopping close to* RAVO, *mockingly)*: Oh you, great thinker, to whom the loveliest girl in the village has been promised; rest your mind a moment, and come celebrate the beauty of the evening with us.

RAVO *(shaking his head)*: Lalatiana is my tomorrow, but the night of drought still separates us. And the shadow of its threats covers our path.

LALATIANA *(stops jumping, too)*: Ravo, your words would make the brave sick with anguish!

192

FALY: You claim, too, that our ancestors are responsible for this blasted drought. Since when do the dead wish harm to the living?

RAVO: Their prohibitions and taboos have become immortal and make us slaves. (*He counts on the fingers of his hand.*) We can't farm the mountainsides because we'd be defiling the tombs; we can't harm the earth with spades but have to burn it like a witch; the forest belongs to man, he can have her like a prostitute . . .

FALY: Oh Ravo, such a wise teacher as you, water flows down from heaven before it reaches the earth; you, too, have the blood of your ancestors in your veins, so why take on the language of another race?

RAVO: Faly, little man, do you really believe that your mother wore her belt too tightly when you were in her belly? Our language must be broadened with the horizon of our time. In the old days, our ancestors followed footpaths, today we have roads.

FALY: You have taken the road a long way; I am still just a dwarf, the plaything of the village who walks on footpaths.

LALATIANA: Stop your bitterness and taste some of nature's honey! Did you notice that luminous curve in the sky? (*She calls and dances.*) The moon is born, an infant without parents, bastard child of the night. Women await her to give birth . . . the cries of newborns will bear the fruit of tenderness.

RAVO: Their mothers won't have enough milk to nurse them: their breasts are as dry as the breast of the earth.

LALATIANA: No! . . . soon the rain will pound down on our soil; the golden grain will blow in the breeze like the treetops when painted by the brushes of the dawn!

RAVO (*putting down his* valiha, *his voice sharp*): Nothing but dreams! . . . stop daydreaming, Lalatiana! Don't you see that even the forest is moved back as if pushed by a gigantic hand? . . . This world is as sad as the look in the eyes of our thirsty children.

FALY (*sits down, he looks weary*): Blanche is thirsty, too. She fled towards the mountain, I had a hard time getting her back . . . poor animal, she's skin and bones. Tonight I'll play my flute to call the rains. (*He takes a flute from his pocket and plays a few notes.*)

LALATIANA (*mockingly*): Your magic flute will awaken the villagers' bad mood: you keep them from sleeping.

FALY: Let them stay up with me. The sounds of my flute will captivate the clouds, and they'll weep with gratitude.

RAVO (*laughs*): You inherited your father's gentle madness. He's convinced that the raindances will bring an end to the drought. They'll take place tomorrow.

LALATIANA: And the Village Chief is calling us together right after. (*She sighs.*) A rather overloaded Sunday!

RAVO (*getting up*): Nature is going to sleep. Come, it's time to fence in the herd.

FALY: Mine is in already, I'm staying.

RAVO: Why? . . . like your white cow, you have to be begged to come home?

FALY: Blanche's mother has a beautiful black coat; there's not a white zebu in the herd; the members of my family are all tall, I'm the only dwarf in the village.

LALATIANA (*impishly*): And the only one who plays a magic flute. Come and sing, charm the night into being our friend.

(FALY *sings accompanied by* RAVO's valiha. *Blackout.*)

SCENE 2

(*The interior of* RAKEVA's *hut.* MAVO *pounds seeds in a small mortar, while* RAKEVA *sharpens a knife.*)

DODA (*standing and gesturing*): The rice plants are dying, the vegetables are scorched . . . where are the miracle workers hiding?

RAKEVA: I wanted to offer a Joro to our ancestors, but everyone acted as if I'd gone mad . . .

DODA: Sacrificing the finest zebu we have when the herd is decimated? I was thinking about the technology of those people you chased away. It's high time they come help us.

RAKEVA: No! . . . their civilization is capable of destroying our planet but can't fight against plagues. They're the ones responsible for this disaster! . . . Tomorrow, our feet, our hands, and our songs will imitate the pounding of the rain. The rites of the ancestors are our first and foremost wealth.

DODA (*bitterly*): The wealth of the starving who stubbornly refuse to use spades and plows and who whisper soft words to an earth that has no ears!

RAKEVA (*pointedly*): That earth feeds us like a mother nurses her child.

MAVO (*imitating her father's tone*): And one day we'll all be sleeping in her belly. (*shouting*) Is that our future? Do we have to spend our lifetime in the shadow of our tombs . . . dust to dust? I've had enough . . . I want to leave, I want to go to the city.

RAKEVA: Be quiet, wretch! Only animals howl like that, you're not a dog baying at the moon!

MAVO (*continuing to yell*): You even refused to let me enjoy the caresses of Lake Androndra . . . water on my skin, in my body, in my dreams! Many went there . . . but we, we stay here, enslaved to this earth that you idolize.

DODA: She's right. Those who moved closer to the lake benefit from an irrigated valley and a beautiful forest.

RAKEVA: You know what they've become? The school-boys of foreigners. Would you like to be ordered around by people you don't know?

DODA: Haga goes there with his wagon, and he's getting rich by selling his barrels of water. The Village Chief's sons go there, too . . . I don't have a wagon.

MAVO: For once, our poverty is a blessing: you'd be merciless like them; you would have swapped water for the life of a child too.

RAKEVA: In a potato field there are always bad roots; if one idiot steals a chicken, why accuse the entire village?

(*We hear* FALY *singing. He comes in, dancing, makes a small bow in front of his father, goes to a trunk and opens it.*

He takes out a lamba[2] *which he throws over his shoulder, makes another bow in front of his father, and goes towards the door.*)

RAKEVA: Where are you going?

FALY: Up by the little wall. I'm going to play the flute to call the rains.

DODA (*indignantly*): Play the flute! . . . we're starving and you're playing the flute! Stop using that little body as an excuse for not growing up.

FALY (*covering his ears*): Don't yell! . . . What good does your yelling do?

DODA: I work! I don't spend my time running after a white cow.

FALY (*in a furious voice*): Blanche is part of the herd!

DODA: . . . and you're part of the family. You have your share of the burden to carry too.

RAKEVA (*intervening*): Leave him alone. It's your poor mother's death that kept him from growing.

MAVO: In that case I should have stayed a little girl, too.

DODA: . . . and me a boy. You'd have had three flute-players up by the wall.

RAKEVA: There wouldn't have been a drought. The birds would have woken us in the morning with their song . . . we would've had plump zebus to give creamy milk to the children you would still be. (*He sighs.*) But time has passed, you've grown up, (*He looks at* FALY.) except for you . . . why?

FALY: Little candles have the same flame as big ones. Does age really have to dry up the fountain of joy?

RAKEVA: The fountain of life is sometimes bitter: Rango's daughter has died, you'll have to represent us at the wake.

FALY: Why me?

DODA and MAVO: Why him?

RAKEVA: Faly must know the face of grief.

(*Blackout.*)

SCENE 3

(*A clearing. The soft light of night. Crickets are heard.* RAVO, *his* valiha *under his arm, enters and calls out.*)

RAVO: Faly! . . . Faly! . . . (*silence*) Faly! . . . answer me, I know you're there.

FALY (*emerging from a dark corner, yawning*): What do you want from me?

RAVO: You're amazing. Why did you leave the wake to sleep here?

FALY (*emphatically*): The wake . . . what wake? Those grimacing faces that reek of wine, all squealing around that little body covered with a sheet . . . is that what a wake is?

RAVO: Those people left their homes to bring comfort to a family in mourning. You have no right to judge them.

FALY: Even if they're behaving like a herd that's gone wild? Can you see yourself under that sheet, your body surrounded by all those bellowing people, discussing arable land, seeding, and cattle?

RAVO: Their carryings-on hide a dreadful and somber song. It's their escape to some imagined consolation.

FALY: The uproar hurts as much as any illness. I dream of a life of serenity in the mountains. The sounds of my flute would welcome the sun, my voice would sing the evening to sleep.

RAVO: Even the forest has changed, Faly. The big trees have disappeared under the ax, the lace-edged palm trees, that used to court the orchids, are no longer there . . . even the birds and the little monkeys have fled. Soon only the reptiles will live there.

FALY: I will fill the silence. The animals will return, I'll be their friend.

RAVO: The friendship of the wild is changeable. Is mine, calm as it may be, no longer enough for you?

FALY: Your knowledge is appreciated everywhere you go. All I am is a stupid child, who can't even manage to lift a sack of rice.

RAVO: Everybody loves you when you sing in the temple.

FALY: Some people have asked me if I exchanged my muscles for a voice.

RAVO: Why worry about it? Envy is an ancient demon, who feels at home wherever he goes.

FALY (*more and more upset*): Did you hear the Pastor's sermon? He was staring at me when he said that Christ didn't need a flute to watch over his herd.

RAVO (*bursts into laughter*): That? That's an angry outburst from someone who needs sleep. Why do you insist on playing your flute at night? (*He softly plays his valiha.*) The soul is a flash of lightning that illuminates the caverns and hollows of life. Sing, Faly, your voice will gnaw away the claws of bitterness, it will hoist you up among the great of this world.

(FALY *sings. Lights and sound dim slowly.*)

SCENE 4

*(The brightly lit stage is bare except for a large boulder.
Insistent drumming is heard. The women carry basins filled
with honey or bunches of bananas on their heads. The men,
dressed in white cloth with red belts, encircle the boulder.
RAVO and the VILLAGE CHIEF standing a little beyond,
watching. RAKEVA raises both hands; silence immediately
follows.)*

RAKEVA: Oh, Zanahary, our Creator, we give thanks to
you for having provided us with feet to walk and with
hands to work. You, our ancestors, you are the source,
we are the rivers, help us to reach the Ocean in which
we shall all be reunited. I am not worthy of speaking,
since I am neither the oldest nor the wisest. Spare me
your wrath . . . bury it seven times the depth of a
man underground, and may the light and the wind
carry my voice towards you. We implore you to help
us, for the clouds have abandoned the sky. Our earth
is no longer fertile, it crumbles and covers us with a
red shroud. We beg for rain! . . . *(He turns to the
listeners.)* Isn't that so, oh people?

THE PEOPLE: May it whip our skin! . . . may it pound
down on our earth! . . . may it nourish our trees and
our crops! . . .

RAKEVA: We wait for the heavens' waters to dry the tears
of our children and to silence the moans of our
women . . . *(to* THE PEOPLE*)* isn't that so, oh people?

THE PEOPLE: May they quench our herds' thirst and
sprout our seeds! . . .

RAKEVA: We hope for a thunder that will make our mountains tremble and for lighting that will stripe our forests like zebras . . . isn't that so, oh people?

THE PEOPLE: May they be the predecessors of water . . . may they herald life to us.

RAKEVA: We watch for heavy and fertile clouds . . . isn't that so, oh people?

THE PEOPLE: May they be as numerous as the birds who criss-crossed the blue above us long ago.

RAKEVA (*crying loudly*): Mangataka orana é![3]

(THE PEOPLE *repeat the phrase in chorus.*)

RAKEVA: Omeo nano é![4]

(THE PEOPLE *repeat the phrase several times as the sounds of the drums begin again, marking the rhythm of the words.*)

RAKEVA (*raising his hands*): Accept our offerings, symbols of our affection and our respect . . . isn't that so, oh people?

(*The women dance around the boulder while pouring honey and placing the bananas.*)

THE PEOPLE: May our life be as sweet as honey . . . may our harvests be as abundant as the fruit of the banana trees.

RAKEVA: Bless our youth, the tree of our future. May they encounter wisdom!

THE PEOPLE: Keep our elders, the framers of our present time.

RAKEVA: Be our guide in this hostile world, oh Zanahary, God of the universe!

THE PEOPLE: Let the water of life flow to us, oh you, our ancestors, sources of our past.

RAKEVA (*crying out*): Omeo orana é![5]

(THE PEOPLE *dance, tirelessly repeating the last phrase. Lights and sound dim.*)

SCENE 5

(A bare room. Sleeping-mats clutter the floor. The whole cast is on stage. The VILLAGE CHIEF *is seated, facing* THE PEOPLE.*)*

THE CHIEF: The shadows stretch eastward. Where are the people of this village? Could they be fearful of reality or do they not even care?

RAVO (*with irony*): They're full of prayers and dances. They're awaiting the miracle that is their right.

RAKEVA (*indignantly*): How dare you be so scornful of our customs? That diploma of yours, that little square of paper you hung in your classroom won't protect you against curses! . . .

DODA: To hell with the cursed and the miraculously cured, let's talk about the drought.

THE CHIEF: It reigns supreme, like an evil sovereign: it denudes the earth, overwhelms the animals, and punishes the people.

MAVO: Do my empty buckets and our parched throats deserve punishment?

THE CHIEF: We have pillaged the forest, burned the land, and chased away the experts.

RAKEVA: I, for one, am proud of that! . . . the forest is ours, burning the land is what we were taught to do by our forefathers, and the experts wanted to experiment here.

RAVO: The forest is our friend, and you don't kill a friend; flames stand for hatred, do you hate our earth? The experts wanted to give us advice; why should we reject every bit of advice because it didn't come from our ancestors?

RAKEVA: Your mind is too young for you to be critical of our experience.

RAVO: The years have plunged you into a bad and heavy sleep; your blindness has attacked your mind . . . and you call that experience!

RAKEVA (*furious*): You're a cock without a spur who cackles like a chicken!

THE CHIEF (*severe*): That's enough; where do you think you are? In a barnyard? Let those who have any suggestions for our survival speak up.

HAGA: Lake Androndra is fifty kilometers away. Do what I do: I go there three times a week to haul water.

MAVO: And you sell it to us for a stiff price, you're just profiteering.

HAGA: You don't really expect me to give it away, do you? I leave the village at dawn and don't get back till night time. I fill my barrels, I keep my nose to the grindstone . . .

LALATIANA: You made Rasoa pay you. Her children haven't had anything to eat so they could have a bit of water.

HAGA: If they survive it's thanks to me. Anyway, the Chief's sons do exactly the same thing, why don't you accuse them?

THE CHIEF: My sons are grown men, it isn't up to me to judge their actions.

DODA: But you do take advantage of their profits!

THE CHIEF: It is their duty to help me.

RAKEVA: Is that why you postponed the raindance?

THE CHIEF: The dance of the fools, yes! . . . you dimwitted minds in caves of superstition, you dare accuse my sons, who are working men!

RAKEVA: Unbeliever! . . . traitor of our traditions!

MAVO: Exploiter of the misery of others!

THE CHIEF: What's stopping you from doing the same?

THE PEOPLE: Hooeeuuuuu!

THE CHIEF: I receive no pay for my function here, I am too old to work . . . my sons have to feed me.

DODA: So leave your seat for a set of younger buttocks.

THE CHIEF: You are the ones who elected me.

THE PEOPLE: No, the ballot boxes were tampered with!

THE CHIEF: That's slander, lies . . .

THE PEOPLE: Hooeeuuuuu!

RAVO (*yelling to quiet the noise*): Be quiet! . . . Come on, quiet down! You are drunk with despair and vengeance and you're making a gentle old man your target. Rage is not a remedy, it's destructive, like lightning.

RANGO (*sadly*): My daughter is to be buried tomorrow. The nurse said she died because there was no water left in her body. I've come here to beg you to save the other children.

(*She bursts into tears and leaves the room. An embarrassed silence follows.*)

FALY (*calls out*): I know! We should requisition all the wagons. The men will take turns going to fetch water from Lake Androndra, and we'll distribute it free of charge.

HAGA (*crudely*): You dwarf, nobody asked you anything, go play your flute!

FALY: You're crude! . . . you just want to keep your profits like the Chief's sons, is that it?

THE CHIEF: You dirty urchin, go suckle your white cow!

DODA: Faly is right! There are five barrels per wagon, that would give us twenty barrels of water per trip.

THE CHIEF: You're wasting your time, the owners will refuse.

LALATIANA: You'll have to force them, after all you represent the law, don't you?

THE CHIEF: We have to respect the property of others.

HAGA: I'll bash in anyone's face who tries to get near my wagon.

DODA: Really? . . .

HAGA: Just try me.

DODA: I won't just try, I'm going to get your wagon. Come, all of you! . . .

HAGA (*He tries to bar their way, shrieking.*): You thieves, you garbage! . . .

DODA: Move over, let us through!

HAGA: No way! . . .

(*They start going at each other. Cries and cursing.*)

THE CHIEF (*trying to separate them*): Stop it, I order you to stop it! (*He is shoved aside.*) Oh, you fools! . . . oh, you poor clowns! (*He is hit and lands flat on the ground.* FALY *wants to help him get up, but the* CHIEF *refuses in a furious voice.*) You dwarf . . . you buffoon! . . . all this is your fault, and you'll pay for it, too, I'm going to call the police.

FALY (*terrified*): The police? . . . Why?

THE CHIEF: To put you in jail, moron! (*He gets up with some difficulty*) Do you hear me? The police will throw you in jail.

FALY (*dumbfounded*): No . . . not the police . . . I don't want to go to jail! . . .

THE CHIEF (*laughs sneeringly*): You're afraid, eh, little man? . . . just as my sons are afraid of losing their profits.

FALY: No, no! . . . (*He shrinks back, the* CHIEF *follows him.*)

THE CHIEF: Oh yes! I'll have you locked up with your cow and your flute!

FALY (*screaming*): No! . . .

THE CHIEF: Yes! . . . (FALY *turns on his heels and runs to the door.*)

LALATIANA (*crying out*): Faly, where are you going? . . . Come back! . . .

DODA (*pushing away his opponent*): What's going on? Where's Faly running off to like that?

MAVO: The Chief wanted to put him in jail. He ran away.

DODA (*to the* CHIEF): Why did you terrorize him? We know the law as well as you.

LALATIANA: He's just showing off his strength against the weakest!

RAKEVA: He's using his position to make himself richer!

THE PEOPLE: Hooeeuuuuu! . . .

RAVO: Fools . . . a pitiful herd of fools, that's what we are. Let's leave this old man in peace. We've got to find Faly before he does something stupid.

DODA: Go with the women, I'm going to call the others to go and get the wagons.

HAGA: Never! . . . you want trouble? You'll have your trouble! . . . (*They exit shoving each other. Blackout.*)

SCENE 6

(MAVO, LALATIANA, *and* RAKEVA *are in the clearing.*)

MAVO and LALATIANA: Faly! . . . Faly! . . .

RAVO (*enters out of breath*): He isn't on the mountain road, I've been there.

LALATIANA: Blanche is in her pen, he would have taken her along.

RAKEVA: His *lamba* and his savings aren't in his trunk anymore. I think he must have gone to the city.

RAVO: I'm going to go after him.

RAKEVA: No, Ravo. He'll appreciate his village once he's far away.

LALATIANA: He thinks he's a fugitive, he's afraid of the police.

RAKEVA: He stayed small because he's been surrounded by friends. Only among strangers will he be forced to grow tall.

(*The* CHIEF *enters, looking very anxious.*)

THE CHIEF: Doda and his friends are threatening to burn the wagons. You have to help me stop them.

SEVERAL VOICES: Lord! . . .

(*Blackout. In semi-darkness,* FALY *crosses the stage, in silhouette, singing a plaintive, nostalgic song.*)

SCENE 7

(*A city street. The sounds of cars, horns, and the hubbub of voices are heard.* RAOZY *is sitting on a stool, selling her rice cakes. A little farther, a blind beggar incessantly repeats the phrase* "mangataka tmpokoi ô." *Pedestrians pass by in different directions.*)

FALY (*dirty and full of dust, approaching* RAOZY): I'd like a cake, please.

RAOZY: That'll be fifty francs.

FALY (*crying out*): That's a lot of money! . . .

RAOZY: I'm not forcing you to buy it.

FALY (*going through his pockets and fishing out a coin*): Here, let me have one, please. (*hesitating*) Why aren't you more polite to me?

RAOZY (*looking at him in astonishment, then bursting out laughing*): Why should I be? Does it bother you?

FALY (*spluttering*): No . . . no, no . . . not at all. (*He takes the cake, sits down in a corner and eats while staring at the passers-by. He wipes his mouth, gets up, and goes back to* RAOZY.) Uh, . . . excuse me . . . I'm thirsty.

RAOZY (*pointing to the audience*): There's a grocery store just across from here. (*maliciously*) The small bottle of fruit juice costs 500 francs.

FALY (*shaking his head*): I'd just like a bit of water.

RAOZY (*pointing upstage*): There's a water-pump.

FALY: Does it cost a lot?

RAOZY (*laughing*): You don't have to pay anything; just turn the faucet, that's all.

FALY (*His face lights up.*): Could I wash myself, too?

RAOZY: As much as you want. (*Sniffs.*) Anyway, you could use it.

(FALY *goes toward the pump. Passers-by cross each other; one or two of them buy a rice cake. The* BEGGAR *continues his litany. Once again,* FALY *comes back to* RAOZY.)

FALY: Tell me, where could I spend the night?

RAOZY: Don't you have a home?

FALY: Oh sure, in my village.

RAOZY: So, go back to your village.

FALY (*flatly*): No.

RAOZY (*shrugging her shoulders*): There are a few hotels . . . the cheapest room costs 2000 francs a night. Do you have a lot of money?

FALY (*taking crumpled bills out of his pocket*): That's it.

RAOZY: Ten thousand francs . . . you'd better go home. (*She stares at two individuals who've come close to* FALY.) And if I were you, I wouldn't show off my money like that, you're going to get mugged. Now, beat it, you're keeping my customers away.

(FALY *moves away, followed by the two individuals. A little further, he sits down and sings, first softly, then more and more loudly. Some passers-by stop to listen. The old* BEGGAR *turns silent, and* RAOZY *steps up on her stool to see him better. At the end of the song, the passers-by applaud and express their approval, showering coins down around him.*)

PASSERS-BY: Bravo!
What a marvelous voice!
Sing some more, little one!
Yeah, something happy!

(FALY, *very proudly, gets up and sings while dancing a few steps. The bystanders clap their hands to the beat. A man in a yellowish uniform, covered with gilded buttons, enters and interrupts.*)

RASOLO: Who gave you permission to sing here? (FALY *falls silent, the crowd scatters.*) Where do you think you are? in a cattle market? . . . You see that building there? Important people are working there, and you're disturbing them. Get the hell out of here, understand? . . .

FALY (*his eyes lowered, trembling*): Yes, Officer, Sir.

(*He moves away, followed once again by the two individuals.*)

RAOZY (*calling the man in uniform*): Hey, Rasolo! . . . you're being promoted awfully fast; first guard, and suddenly police officer! . . .

RASOLO (*imitating a military salute*): My cap is as good as a kepi, isn't it? . . . (*They both laugh.* FALY *comes downstage and looks straight ahead, distraught. The two individuals approach him.*)

FIRST ROBBER: Can we help you?

FALY: I was trying to cross the street, but there's too much traffic. (*He takes a step forward and shrinks back just as quickly.*)

SECOND ROBBER: You can't cross here; come, over there are lights.

FALY (*Looking in all directions*): Lights? . . . Where do you see lights?

FIRST ROBBER: You're a great guy! We'll give you a place to stay. In return, you'll sing for us . . . you've got a great voice.

FALY: Really? Sure, I'd like that.

RAOZY (*She has been watching the moves of the two men, and cries out.*): Hey you . . . hey, you, farmboy, don't go along with them!

SECOND ROBBER (*threateningly*): Hey girl, shut up and sell your cakes.

(RAOZY *lowers her head. They exit. Blackout.*)

SCENE 8

(*Morning light in the street.* FALY, *curled up in a corner, is asleep on the ground. The* BLIND BEGGAR *enters, feeling his way with a cane, sits down and starts his litany. A passer-by drops a coin in his hat, the* BEGGAR *thanks him profusely in Malagasy.* RAOZY *enters, carrying her stool, a mat, a basin full of rice cakes, and gets settled.* RASOLO, *the guard, stands in front of the door.*)

RAOZY: Good morning, Rasolo, you okay?

RASOLO: Yeah, I didn't sleep, it's like a jungle here at night. (*He goes toward* RAOZY *and hands her a coin*): Give me a cake, I'm hungry.

FALY (*sits up, rubs his eyes, sees* RASOLO *and jumps up, crying*): Officer, Sir! . . . Officer, Sir! . . .

RASOLO (*checking around with a worried look*): Hey, take it easy little one, I'm no police officer.

FALY (*disappointed*): You're not the police?

RASOLO: Well . . . no, I'm a guard. Why do you insist that I be the police?

FALY: I was waiting for you . . . I was hoping you'd help me. They stole everything from me: my flute, my *lamba,* and my money.

RAOZY: Didn't I warn you, why did you tag along with those hoodlums?

FALY: I didn't know they were thieves, they were so nice to me. (*clutching his stomach*) . . . I'm hungry! . . .

RAOZY: Do you want a cake?

FALY (*holding out his hand*): Oh yes, thank you.

RAOZY: That'll be fifty francs.

FALY (*pulls his hand back*): My money's gone.

RASOLO (*his mouth full*): You ought to see the police.

FALY: Where can I find them?

RASOLO (*points to the audience*): Cross the street, take the second left, and the next right. Then go straight, there's a traffic circle, then you . . .

FALY (*shaking his head*): I'll never find it; please come with me.

RASOLO: I've been working all night, my wife's waiting for me. The cops will ask you questions; do you have any witnesses?

FALY: They robbed me in an alley . . . but I'd recognize them, and the lady here saw them, too . . .

RAOZY (*interrupting quickly*): Those hoodlums will murder us if we turn them in . . . forget them and find some work.

FALY (*proudly*): I'm not afraid of them.

RASOLO (*laughing at him, as he looks him up and down*): Well, well, well . . .

RAOZY: I am afraid. Please, I beg you, let it go. Find some work.

FALY: Sure, fine. Where should I go to find work?

RASOLO (*sounding important*): What can you do? Do you have any diplomas?

FALY: No. Ravo, the teacher, taught me to read. I know how to herd cattle.

RAOZY (*cries out*): But there're no herds in a city!

FALY (*pointing at the audience*): What about them?

RASOLO (*bursts out laughing*): Those people are waiting for the bus.

FALY: It looks like a herd to me.

RASOLO: You little rascal! . . . just tell them that . . . you'll be in trouble, that's for sure.

FALY: In my village, water is a treasure; here, every faucet is a spring. We share our cakes, you sell them dearly. We hope for rain, you wait for the bus . . . what pasture are you going to?

RASOLO: What's that?

FALY: It's an immense space where the wind blows through the bushes, where the herds graze so they can give milk to the children and meat to the adults.

RASOLO: We buy rice and meat with the money we make when we work.

FALY: . . . or you beg and steal. You've got a bad herdsman.

RASOLO (*annoyed*): Stop comparing us to your cattle! . . . We don't need that here.

FALY: Oh yes, you do. Your city feeds off the cattle we breed and off our harvests.

RAOZY: He's right; there's no way I could make cakes without rice. I've spent all my life behind four dirty walls and in this street. (*thoughtfully*) I'd love to see a pasture . . . is your village far away?

FALY: I walked for two days and two nights.

RAOZY (*ironically*): And why did you leave that paradise of yours to come be with beggars and thieves?

FALY (*looking off into the distance*): The wind has chased the clouds away. It was jealous of the rain making the land fertile . . . the sun sucked up the least little drop that hid near the plants' roots. Everything was veiled in red: the village, the pasture . . . even Blanche had become red.

RASOLO (*tapping his finger against his temple*): This little guy's crazy. He talks like a poet though he barely knows how to read.

FALY: Words come from the spirit, which is wisdom's eye. My father has never written a single letter, and yet people listen to him.

RASOLO: Well, let him eat that then while he waits for the rain. Here, the only difference we know is between day and night. We eat without worrying about the weather . . . (*he moves away*) see you tonight.

FALY (*groaning*): I'm hungry.

(RAOZY *hands him a cake.*)

FALY: Thank you. What's your name?

RAOZY: Raozy, and like the flower, I've lost my petals.

FALY: Plants need light and attention to blossom. My name is Faly.

RAOZY: I'd like to learn to talk like you do.

FALY: Words are alive, you have to love them. They can make us dirty or make us great. Where I come from, men test their skill by debating one another and women are judged by how they use the language.

RAOZY: Here, all we worry about is our stomach.

FALY (*laughs*): We've got that too, but it doesn't upset us.

RAOZY (*laughs also*): Really? . . . and what will you fill your stomach with? You see the woman there, carrying that load? Go help her carry her baskets. She'll give you some money.

(FALY *runs over and grabs one of the baskets from the woman passing by.*)

FALY: Let me give you a hand.

THE WOMAN (*squealing*): Let go of my basket! . . . will you let go of my basket, you dirty little thief!

FALY (*draws back, catching his breath*): I wasn't trying to steal from you . . . I wanted . . .

THE WOMAN: Get away or I'll call the police!

FALY (*trembling*): The police . . . (*He stumbles back near* RAOZY) She wanted to call the police! . . .

RAOZY: You have to ask for permission first before you even get close to them. There are a lot of thieves here.

FALY: But why?

RAOZY: The starving, hoodlums, good-for-nothings . . . don't you have thieves where you come from?

FALY: We all know each other. Will you come with me when I go back to the village?

RAOZY (*flirtatiously*): Is that a marriage proposal?

FALY (*stammers*): No . . . well, yes . . . you're very sweet . . .

RAOZY (*smiles*): Is that all? Have you forgotten your pretty lines? (*pushes his elbow*) Look, a man with two suitcases. Go, but careful, first ask him politely if he'll let you help him.

FALY (*goes over to the man*): Sir, may I give you a hand in exchange for a bit of money?

(*Cries burst forth: "Catch the thief! . . . Catch the thief! . . ." The man drops his suitcases at* FALY's *feet.*)

THE MAN: Here, you can have them. (*He runs away. A woman enters, gesturing wildly.*)

WOMAN PLAINTIFF: There they are! my suitcases . . . Catch the thief! . . . Get him! . . . (*Two men who follow her, grab* FALY *and begin to beat him up.*)

THE MEN: You bastard, you dirty little thief! . . .

RAOZY (*jumping up and shouting*): Stop that! . . . that's not the thief! . . . (*The two men continue beating* FALY, *who crumples under their blows.*)

RAOZY (*shrieks*): Come on, you've got to stop! you're going to kill an innocent . . .

ONE OF THE MEN: So you're in it with him, eh?

RAOZY: I'm a witness!

BLIND BEGGAR: Me too!

AN ONLOOKER (*snickering*): What did you see, blindman?

RAOZY: You're the ones who are blind . . . blind and deaf . . . a herd of invalids! . . . don't hit him any more! . . . Let him go.

ONE OF THE MEN: He's a thief, he's going to pay for this.

RAOZY (*standing between them*): Are you the law? Are you the judge?

ONE OF THE MEN: Enough, enough, let's go to the police station. (*They pull* FALY *up roughly.*)

RAOZY: He's hurt, he needs help.

ONE OF THE MEN (*snickering*): Is this your man?

RAOZY: He's my fiancé. I'm going with you.

BLIND BEGGAR: Go ahead and don't worry, I'll sell your cakes for you. (*They exit. The* BLIND BEGGAR *sits down on* RAOZY's *stool*) Come and buy my cakes! . . . Come and buy my cakes! . . . They're sweet as honey! . . . Come and buy my cakes! . . . (*Blackout.*)

SCENE 9

(RAVO *and* LALATIANA *are in the clearing. Sounds of far-off thunder are heard.*)

RAVO: Did you hear that?

LALATIANA: It's thunder . . . Why?

RAVO (*jumping up suddenly*): Why? . . . but that's the rain! . . . streams of rain! Waterfalls of rain! . . .

LALATIANA (*raising her hands to the sky*): Come down . . . come down to us, oh, you drops of life . . . beat against our bodies, whip the earth!

MAVO (*enters running*): The clouds are hiding the rising of the sun! . . . the sky is zebra-striped with lightning . . . the storm is coming closer to us, it's coming straight at us!

(*The three young people, mad with joy, dance and sing the words of the raindance song at the top of their lungs. RAKEVA enters. MAVO wants to pull him into their dance; the old man shakes his head and shows them a letter.*)

MAVO: A letter?

RAKEVA: Yes, from the city.

RAVO (*happily*): Has Faly written us?

RAKEVA: No, it's from a woman. Faly has been hurt, and he's in prison.

RAVO, MAVO, and LALATIANA (*anxiously*): In prison!

RAKEVA: He's been accused of stealing. Some passers-by beat him up and dragged him to the police station.

RAVO, MAVO, and LALATIANA (*indignantly*):
That's slander!
Faly is no thief!
How badly hurt is he?
Who's the woman of the letter?

RAKEVA: Her name is Raozy, she's Faly's fiancée.

RAVO, MAVO and LALATIANA (*incredulously*): His fiancée! . . . (*They look at each other in shock.*)

RAKEVA: It's normal, he's twenty-six.

RAVO: We have to help him!

RAKEVA (*bitterly*): The experts are invading our village, their machines are hurting our soil . . . I don't want to watch that anymore, I'm going to look for my son.

MAVO: I'm coming with you.

RAKEVA (*flatly*): No, I'm going to try to get my son out of prison. I don't want to have to pick my only daughter off some sidewalk in the city. Go help Doda with the sowing.

RAVO: I'm going with you. It's vacation time.

RAKEVA: Come along them. I don't know the city, nor its people. You tell them that Faly belongs to an honorable family. They'll let him go.

LALATIANA: May I come?

RAKEVA: If you want to. Your fiancé will guarantee your return to the village.

(Blackout.)

SCENE 10

(*The* POLICE INSPECTOR, *in uniform, sits behind a desk in his office.* FALY, *with a huge bandage on his head and his arm in a sling, sits facing the desk. The* WOMAN PLAINTIFF *sits upstage. Standing in the back of the room are* RAKEVA, RAOZY, LALATIANA, *and* RAVO, *his inseparable* valiha *under his arm.*)

POLICE INSPECTOR (*reading a file*): Your name is Faly Rakeva, you're twenty-six years old, and you raise cattle. You left your village, Befotaka, because drought and famine threatened the village. Is that correct?

FALY (*stammering*): Yes . . . no . . . Officer, Sir.

POLICE INSPECTOR: I'm not an officer, but the Inspector . . . Police Inspector. So, is it yes or is it no?

FALY: I ran away from the village because the village Chief wanted to put me in jail. (*dismayed murmurs*)

POLICE INSPECTOR: Tell me about that. What did you steal?

FALY: Nothing, Sir Police. I only suggested that we requisition the wagons to go and get water from Lake Androndra.

POLICE INSPECTOR (*irritated*): I am the Inspector, do you hear me? Police Inspector. The village Chief wanted to have you put in jail because you stole those wagons . . . Admit it!

RAVO (*intervenes*): Inspector, Sir, let me . . .

POLICE INSPECTOR (*violently*): Be quiet! . . . You'll answer me when I ask you something! . . . (*to* FALY) So you left your village to continue your thievery in the city?

FALY: No, Sir. Rango's daughter had died of thirst; Rasoa's children didn't have anything to eat just so they could have a drop of water . . . so, I thought it was a good idea to suggest requisitioning the wagons . . . but Ravo, Doda, and Haga started fighting . . . The Chief became very angry and wanted to call the police . . . I was frightened and ran away. In town, I followed two men who'd offered me a place to stay; they stole everything I had. I wanted to see you, Sir Police, but there were too many cars, I was afraid to cross the street . . . I was hungry; Raozy offered me some cakes. I wanted to find some work, but there are no herds in the city. (*He stops and looks around him, in every direction.*)

POLICE INSPECTOR (*kindly*): Go on, I'm listening.

FALY: I wanted to help a man carry his suitcases to earn a bit of money. He left them right near me and ran off . . . two men beat me up . . . I was locked up in a dark room with some very big men, it was stifling . . . there wasn't any sun, it was dark all the time . . . I am no thief, Sir Police, I don't want to go back in that black pen with that herd of shadows . . . My father told that the rain has returned and that we have spades and plows. It's the sowing season, there's much work to do in my village, please, I beg you . . . let me go home. Blanche must be waiting for me.

POLICE INSPECTOR: Who is Blanche?

FALY: She's the only white cow in the herd, just as I'm the only dwarf in the village. But she was smarter than me, she stayed right with the herd . . . and if she hadn't, what would have become of her?

POLICE INSPECTOR (*dreamily*): Is your village far away?

RAOZY: It's two days and two nights walking. I'm going there, Mr. Inspector. I don't want to live five to a room anymore at night, and on some street corner during the day. The sun will play on my skin, the shade of the leaves will protect me when I sleep . . . I'll go to the wide-open pasture with Blanche . . . I'll no longer be part of the herd of city-people, whose only herdsman is money.

POLICE INSPECTOR: You're a lucky woman and you speak very well. Who taught you how to express yourself like that?

RAOZY: Faly told me to choose my words with care, since words are alive. You can make a bouquet of words to give to those you love or a herd of words to groan its hatred.

POLICE INSPECTOR (*turning to the* WOMAN PLAINTIFF): Madam, do you wish to pursue your accusations against Faly Rakeva? Do you recognize him as your thief?

WOMAN PLAINTIFF (*hesitatingly*): Eh . . . no . . . the thief was much bigger . . . and, anyway, this little guy could never have carried my suitcases. They're quite heavy.

FALY (*indignantly*): Do you take me for a little kid? I sure can carry your suitcases! . . .

RAKEVA, RAOZY, LALATIANA and RAVO (*horrified*): Be quiet, Faly! . . . be quiet! . . .

FALY: I won't be quiet, I'm not a little kid! . . .

POLICE INSPECTOR (*laughing*): Calm down, Faly, a few inches less than others is really not a handicap. (*in an official voice*) Faly Rakeva, in view of the fact that the plaintiff does not recognize you as the thief of her suitcases, your case is closed. You are free to go.

FALY (*crying out*): Free to go back to the village? . . . to grow rice? . . . to watch over my herd . . . and to play the flute by the little wall?

RAOZY (*tenderly, going to him*): Yes, Faly, and I'll be by your side.

FALY (*rushing to* RAVO): Yes, yes, of course . . . but I have to thank Sir Police first.

POLICE INSPECTOR (*energetically*): No . . . no . . . you don't owe me a thing, I've only done my duty.

FALY (*feverishly, not listening to him*): Do you have your *valiha*, Ravo?

RAVO: Yes, why?

FALY (*jubilantly*): Well then, play! I want to sing for Mr. Police.

POLICE INSPECTOR: No, not here . . . this is a police station!

FALY: Is singing forbidden in a police station?

POLICE INSPECTOR: No, but . . .

FALY: Well, I want to sing for you to thank you. Play, Ravo.

(RAVO *plays his* valiha. FALY *sings*.)

POLICE INSPECTOR (*begging*): Not so loud . . . not so loud . . . the Commissioner is working, and I'm going to be held responsible! . . . (*A man dressed in a three-piece suit stands in the doorway.*)

COMMISSIONER: What a magnificent voice!

POLICE INSPECTOR (*deferentially*): Isn't it though, Commissioner?

COMMISSIONER: What's the name of their village?

POLICE INSPECTOR: Befotaka, Sir.

COMMISSIONER (*nodding*): I know it, it's a lovely place. The police sergeant is a friend of mine. One day we'll go and visit them.

FALY (*stops singing, and calls out*): No, no policemen, Mr. Police . . . no policemen, please!

(*Bursts of laughter, the sounds of* valihas. *Curtain.*)

Translator's Notes:

[1]The *valiha* is the name commonly used in Madagascar for the tube zither. It is one of the oldest of the Malagasy instruments and originated in South-East Asia. Although there are several types, the valiha is usually made from a bamboo cane which serves as a direct resonator with sections of unequal length at each end; the end sections amplify the sound.

[2]The *lamba* is a garment much like a poncho, worn by men.

[3]We beg for rain.

[4]Give us water.

[5]Give us rain.

Josué Kossi Efoui was born in Togo in 1962. He received degrees in English and Philosophy from the University of Benin in Lomé, Togo. An actor as well as writer, he performed with the troupe from the French Cultural Center, and the Nivaquine and Koliko Company, both in Lomé, from 1986 to 1989. *The crossroads (Le Carrefour)* was first performed by the Nivaquine and Koliko company at the Lomé French Cultural Center in 1988. It was awarded first prize in Radio France Internationale's 1989 Inter-African Theatre Competition and was published in the journal *Théâtre Sud* (no. 2, 1990). In 1990, the same company performed his play *La Récupération* at the Lomé French Cultural Center. Efoui's short story, *Indépendence cha-cha sur fond de Blues*, published by Canadia Mondia, won first prize in the first African Short Story Competition in 1990. His short story, *Est-il déjà porté disparu?*, and an essay, *A quoi sert la philosophie?* have both been published in the journal *Propos Scientifiques* (nos. 7 and 9, 1988). Efoui produced a literary program on Radio Lomé Togo in 1989.

Jill Mac Dougall has been directly involved in theater research and production in France, Zaire, the Ivory Coast, and Quebec for over twenty years. Since 1979, she has been translating works of French-speaking writers such as Marc Sauvageon, Anne Legault, Lise de Vaillancourt, and Marco Micone. Her translations of Diur N'Tumb's *Lost Voices* and Bernard Zadi Zaourou's *The Eye* are included in Ubu Repertory Theater's first *Afrique* anthology and her translation of Abla Farhoud's *The Girls from the Five and Ten* and Fatima Gallaire Bourega's *You Have Come Back* were published in Ubu's anthology *Plays by Women*. Her translation of Jean-Pol Fargeau's *Burn River Burn* is included in Ubu's anthology, *Theater and Politics*. Mac Dougall is also a scholar and critic who specializes in cross-cultural performance. She is presently writing a book on performing identities in Quebec.

The premiere of the English translation of *The Crossroads* was directed in a staged reading by Fred Tyson at Ubu Repertory Theater on May 2, 1991.

CHARACTERS

THE PROMPTER
THE WOMAN
THE POET
THE COP

(The stage represents a crossroads. An unlit street lamp stands in the middle. There is a bench in the corner. At the back of the stage is a podium with a music stand where the PROMPTER *stands. There is also a large jar of water the* WOMAN *uses to tell the future.*

The PROMPTER *enters. This character is similar to a master of ceremonies or a puppeteer. At his signal, the street lamp lights up. Another gesture and the stage lights come on, revealing the* WOMAN *who is lying in a contorted position, like an abandoned string puppet. Using gestures and signals, the* PROMPTER *attempts to reanimate her. Suddenly she lets out a cry.)*

WOMAN: What's happening to me? This is so odd. It feels like . . . No. And yet . . . This feels so strange. I have the impression I've already lived through this scene. One night, exactly like this one. I stepped on this same stage. In these same lights. On this same set. And, I moved downstage as I'm doing now, and, exactly like the other time, I . . . Yes, like the other time . . . I forgot my lines.

PROMPTER: Yet it is . . .

WOMAN: Yet it is the first time this has ever happened to me. Like so many things that happen only once but seem to have happened seven times over . . . When my friend Rachel died, I had lived through it all before. I relived it exactly as I am today. Like something starting over. That pain that hardens the throat like a lump of nausea, and the eyes like . . . like . . . No, it doesn't even hurt anymore, a pain like that doesn't even leave a wound. Not the slightest scratch on the belly. Not even a cramp. Not even a twinge. Not even . . . a wrinkle. It seems so stupid: you're innocently thumbing through the paper one day, and all of a sudden you come across "a young woman had her legs crushed in an automobile accident this morning at 10 a.m. . . ." And you refuse to recognize the young woman in the picture there in front of you. What the driver doesn't know is that "a young woman" is named Rachel, that she has a friend, that the evening of the accident someone might have made love to her and told her what beautiful legs she had. And that she is in love. What they don't know, all of those who are now telling her, "Thank God you're still alive" is that she is in fact dead. Because her life was dancing. Rachel is a friend of the best kind, the type you can say unpleasant things to when she happens by, just because you're in a lousy mood.

(*A pause. The actress remains immobile, apparently stuck.*)

PROMPTER: This peculiar . . . This peculiar . . .

(*The* WOMAN *does not react. The* PROMPTER *sets her into motion again with a gesture.*)

WOMAN: This peculiar feeling. There it is again . . . Just as it was a long time ago, when that other one left, because he couldn't stand it here anymore, living in this desert, at these crossroads where all the paths are full of traps, where you can't move anymore than you can sit down, stand up, or sleep, or scream, or weep, or die. You can never get far enough to escape. It's true, but he did manage to leave, to escape from the

crossroads where only this street lamp burns, burns
time itself, the time of a one act in a few short scenes.
Or maybe two acts. Maybe three. He left a long time
ago. (*She goes to the water jar where she looks into the
future.*) But tonight he will come back. He'll stay the
time of the play. One act in a few scenes. Or maybe
two or maybe three. He'll say this is the reason he's
come. To act the play. And we will pretend not to
recognize each other. We will act as in the theatre. We
will be natural.

(*A pause. The* PROMPTER *signals. The* POET *enters and
freezes.*)

There he is. It's really him. He's come from so
far . . . He was always part of another world, a
disappearing species, a race of travelers, explorers,
searchers.

(*At the* PROMPTER's *signal, the* POET *steps forward.*)

He will come and he'll ask me . . .

POET: Are you from here?

(*She appears amazed. She turns her head slowly toward the
POET, lets out a scream and backs away.*)

WOMAN: You scared me.

POET: I'm sorry. I'm trying to find my way.

WOMAN: You too?

POET: What do you mean, me too?

WOMAN: I think I passed a man coming here. He was also trying to find his way . . .

POET: There are fewer and fewer who are trying to find their way. But there are more and more guides and beacons. I've seen quite a few beacons. There was a tiny one that blinked steadily as if it were the eye of the universe. I saw one way up high that gave no light but made me dizzy. There was another one, quite famous and brilliant, that called out, "Come, come, I'll give you the light." But anybody who went too close came back blinded . . . by the light. So many thought they were rare specimens that you can't take them seriously anymore. You can hardly tell the king from the jester these days.

WOMAN: I was saying I'd met a man who had lost his way. He seemed very distrustful. He changed into a shadow to better disappear into the woodwork. He tried to find his way without even asking anyone. Here they don't like people asking questions. Remember that. If you're looking for your way, just walk straight on, and if you have the bad luck to run into a policeman, don't be so foolish as to ask him. Do you have a mask?

POET: A mask?

WOMAN: Yes, a gas mask. You don't have a gas mask?

POET: No.

WOMAN: This doesn't look good at all.

POET: Why?

WOMAN: They have tear gas. There are riots in the streets, fights, murders. Some people have a price on their heads. (*to audience*) How can I tell him he's wanted, that they've been looking for him since he left? (*At a signal from the* PROMPTER *she turns back to the* POET.) Do you have a helmet?

POET: No. Why?

WOMAN: They have clubs. You have to protect your head these days. It's the law. Any policeman will tell you that. But what they don't tell you is you also have to protect your . . . (*She looks around cautiously and then points to her behind.*) But that's not required by law. Just by experience. A kick in the ass can happen so easily. Well, good-bye then. (*She holds out her hand but then draws it back abruptly.*)

POET: Do I still frighten you?

WOMAN: A little.

POET: Is it my bag that scares you?

WOMAN: A little, yes . . . it's odd. It looks like . . . wait . . . like a hunter's game bag . . . a headhunter's bag. (*They laugh.*)

POET: When I crossed the thousandth roadblock, a cop told me: "That is a bag of tricks." (*They laugh. Embarrassed silence. False smiles. Hesitations.*) Are you from around here?

WOMAN: I'm from the crossroads. (*pause*) Is it really sunny where you just came from? Sun rising all morning? Sun setting all evening? Flowers blooming in all seasons? Where you just came from . . .

POET: There's death and fear in the air too.

WOMAN: Here, there are no flowers because there are no seasons, because there is no sun. Only this street lamp marks the night. Nothing else. Not even the seeds we sow. Not even the roots we bear. I'm looking for a softer country.

POET: I was looking for a softer country.

WOMAN: Over there . . .

POET: Fog. It's strange.

WOMAN: There's death in the air here too. And disaster. Adventurers throw themselves headfirst into death. Travelers don't stay long and they never come back. (*pause*) Why did you come back?

POET (*He looks around, embarrassed.*): I'm not from here. I'm just passing through. (*She smiles as if to say "You can't fool me."*) Good-bye. (*He holds out his hand, which she takes a moment and then turns over to read his palm. She*

245

looks at him and then opens her mouth to speak. He runs out. She follows.)

WOMAN (*shouting*): Where are you going? Put on a clown mask so you won't be recognized. They're looking for . . . (*She clasps her hand over her mouth.*) I recognized him immediately by his palm. It's him, it's really him. I know he recognized me too. (*She runs after him. The stage is empty for a moment. She reappears from the opposite wing. She seems disoriented.*) What can we do about these crossroads. It's a real labyrinth. It's full of dead ends. He is lost. Lost . . . lost . . . (*She is about to exit when the* POET *appears behind her.*)

POET: Here I am. For an act with a few scenes. Maybe a second act. Or a third. Then I'll leave.

WOMAN: Yes, it really is you. Come here, come let me get a look at you. (*She pulls him over to the street lamp.*) Indeed, it's you. The same eyes demanding to see, the same mouth asking all the day long "Why this? Why that?" I was only a bit older than you. One day you asked me . . . (*He puts his finger on her mouth.*) Okay, I won't say it. (*pause*) But one day you wanted to know . . . (*He gives her an angry look. She bursts out laughing. He also laughs. Suddenly she is sad. Silence.*)

POET: I know what you're thinking.

WOMAN: I knew you'd leave one day. That you'd never get used to living in this dead end. You weren't born under the sign of the chameleon like most people around here. You never learned to fade into the scenery. Gray doesn't suit you; your skin refuses the dullness. (*She takes his hand and reads the lines.*) You were born to weave your web and remain naked. You were born under the sign of the spider, born to nakedness. Your naked truth. One day you came to me and said . . .

POET (*Turning his back, he moves away.*): I'm leaving.

WOMAN (*to herself*): You're leaving . . .

POET: I'm not happy here.

WOMAN (*to herself again*): You're not happy here.

POET: I'd like to find a way out of the crossroads.

WOMAN: Out of the crossroads.

POET (*turning to her*): And you didn't understand. In your mind it was escape and denials. Why would I run away from you? You know, this business . . . (*She puts her finger on his lips. He pulls away slowly.*) You didn't understand me.

WOMAN: But I did. I understood you couldn't stay too long sitting down or standing up, lying or dying, without getting stiff. So you start moving around so much that they notice you. They don't like that, here. Everyone should remain still in this mass grave. Dead.

POET: Then why . . .

247

WOMAN (*mechanically*): Why did you come back?

POET: Over there I'm the foreigner.

WOMAN: And here?

POET (*mechanically*): I'm the foreigner.

WOMAN: Here I feel exactly like you do over there. Yet
I'm here.

POET: I'm the foreigner.

WOMAN: Stop it.

POET: Over there my sleep was erratic. I was crumbling.
I see a woman coming toward me. I hold out my
hand. She walks through me and moves on. I was a
ghost. I even scared people. Over there I am the
other.

WOMAN: And here?

POET: One morning over there I realized mold was
growing on my hands that no one had held for a long
time. And grass was growing in my heart, thick,
opaque. It started to blind me . . .

WOMAN: And gradually, insidiously, it began to think
for you.

POET: So I came back. If I had stayed I would always
have been the foreigner.

WOMAN: And here? Here you're the outlaw. The Pariah.

POET: Outlaw. Pariah. Outlaw. Pariah. Outlaw. Pariah.

WOMAN: What are you doing?

POET: I'm repeating so I won't forget. So when a cop asks me "Who are you?" I can stand at attention and shout "Outlaw, Sir. Pariah, Sir." Like that cop I met just before . . . (*As he speaks the* PROMPTER *signals and the* COP *enters. The* WOMAN *glances over the* POET's *shoulder and sees the* COP.)

WOMAN: Oh, no.

POET: Yes.

WOMAN: You met a cop on your way?

POET: Of course.

WOMAN: My God, what was he like?

POET: Classic.

WOMAN: Leather boots?

POET: Leather boots.

WOMAN: The color of iron?

POET: The color of rust.

WOMAN: A club?

POET: A club.

WOMAN: And his head? Square?

POET: Square with . . .

WOMAN: With . . .

POET: A headband . . .

WOMAN: A headband, oh God, a headband . . . and it was . . .

POET: It was . . .

WOMAN and POET (*together*): Red. (*Silence.*)

WOMAN: Did he recognize you?

POET: Why should he recognize me?

WOMAN: Don't you know there's a price on your head? (*The* POET *opens his mouth: no sound.*) We have to hurry. Go sit over there in the shadows. I'll take care of him.

COP (*sniffing the air*): It smells suspect here.

(*The* WOMAN *approaches him and does a seductive number. Gestures. She manages to draw the* COP *away.*)

POET: Suspect. Suspect. There's that word again. As far back as I can remember, it's the same old story. Nostrils flaring like a bulldog smelling bad meat. Suspect. Like my friend the painter. He was classified suspect too. Because he used to draw pictures that people didn't always understand. So the cops would raid his place from time to time. They would tear up his books and notes and slash his paintings. Since they never found anything there, they started searching inside him, cutting him into little pieces. We'd see the painter after that, busy gluing himself back together, remolding, replastering his body. I was a child. I watched. He said it was to intimidate him they'd done that. I asked him, "Sir, what does intimidate mean?" One day he came back and discovered that among the pieces he'd gathered and started gluing together, he couldn't find his tongue. And that was it. He'll never say another word. Not a single word. He can only smile. He's the one who taught me how to smile and even to laugh, laugh about anything, about myself, my mistakes, my misfortunes. He taught me how to smile. He said that only real smiles count. A smile doesn't lie. You can't smile cynically or cruelly. That's just a grimace, nothing more. You roll up your lips like you roll up your sleeves to start beating some-body. No one is fooled. He taught me to see too. He had eyes made to see. The enormous eyes of a poet, big as oceans. And full of things. And cloudy. When they looked at you, you felt transparent. He taught me to see through opaque and closed surfaces, to turn things inside out. They didn't like his eyes here. They found them suspect. They said his eyes were gadgets for spying, hidden cameras, witch's eyes, the eyes of a

WOMAN: He was born here like you, but you can't know what he's known, what he's been through to be bruised to the bone. You can't imagine what it's like to wake up on a sunny morning and to clash head on with a long and narrow day like a closed tunnel . . . You shut your door and you return to your night. And you go back and forth with this feeling of closed doors inside you. Sealed air-tight. And behind these closed doors there are things that lost their names, things that peck at you, that gnaw away your insides like acid. Everything feels like erosion. Erosion.

COP: Is that why he left?

WOMAN: You don't know what they put him through . . . He felt a quivering through his pores. So he saved a few dreams, the older ones; he saved them from the erosion by hiding them in poems, by changing them into music. He carved them in ebony, in stone, anything that has a hard memory. He felt a quivering, a desire, a call from somewhere else. So he escaped, taking a few of his lighter dreams.

COP: Let him talk for himself. Why did you leave?

POET: I felt a quivering in my pores, desires, calls from elsewhere . . .

COP: Just a second here. I think I already heard that somewhere. And what kind of way is that to talk . . . quivering . . . desires . . . calls . . . First of all who's calling you, huh? Who are you working for?

WOMAN: He's a poet. Give him another chance.

COP: No, he smells suspect.

WOMAN: Listen to me. He's come back this evening to play out his last scene.

PROMPTER: His last chance.

WOMAN: Give him the chance to be himself by pretending. Day will break when the street lamp goes out, and you can take him away. Just an evening to . . . to . . . I don't know what to say.

PROMPTER: To exist.

WOMAN: To exist for himself.

COP: No. I don't understand a word of your script. The only script I was given is the law. It's simple, just two things: "You will arrest and you will condition."

WOMAN: What does condition mean?

COP: It means get into shape.

WOMAN: Which means?

COP: Prepare a suspect so that he will collaborate during the interrogation. Develop a sense of guilt in the suspect so that he will agree to a . . .

PROMPTER: Dialogue.

COP: A dialogue, you know, so he'll answer questions the way we want. Yes when it's yes and no when it's no. In other words, no lying. For example, you arrest a suspect. You show him a file that proves he's guilty, information we've spent a hell of a long time fabricating. And you know what that son of a bitch says: "I won't sign. I'm innocent." As if we hadn't already smelled him out, as if the police could be wrong. So what are we supposed to do? We have to soften him up, get him into shape, push him to the limits, starve him, keep him from sleeping. That's conditioning. And when he's conditioned what do you think he does? He confesses and then he signs.

WOMAN: They used to call that the third degree. It's an ancient method.

COP: Well, we call it conditioning. And we've got electric current. Isn't progress wonderful? A few wires in the right places, a few sharp little shocks and the jig is up.

(*As if sleepwalking, the* POET *moves to the* COP *and takes him by the neck.*)

POET: His eyes were like oceans . . . He could see things from all sides . . . Conditioning . . . so it was you . . . conditioning . . . Cut out the tongue, gouge out the eyes . . . It was the likes of you . . .

(*Laughing, the* COP *strikes the* POET *who collapses. The* COP *turns him over with a kick.*)

COP: Say, I like this guy. We're going to have fun. Okay, let's get on with this. Enough time wasted.

255

WOMAN (*clutching the* COP*'s arm*): Just one more chance.

COP: No.

WOMAN: Just one more . . . (*lascivious*) And I'll give you . . . three.

COP: No. Attempted corruption.

WOMAN (*same tone*): I'll give you four chances.

COP (*less convinced*): No.

WOMAN: Five.

COP: Five? Let me think . . . six.

WOMAN: All right, six.

COP: You know I can't refuse you anything. Okay, he's all yours but remember when the street lamp goes out, when day breaks, then the show is over. I'm taking him away. But when do we meet for . . .

PROMPTER: For . . . (*meaningful cough*)

COP: For . . . (*meaningful cough*)

WOMAN: Whenever you want.

(*The* COP *goes to stretch out on the bench.*)

COP: Six to one, not a bad deal. Since I'll nab him in the end anyway.

WOMAN (*to the* POET): And now you can stop performing on a stage where nobody understands what you're saying. Tonight you can tell the truth because you know you're condemned. He won't leave you alone. I can't stop him; he has his own role to play. But I can hold him back. And that's what I did.

POET: At what price.

WOMAN: I had no choice. And I've never had a choice. I was born with no choice.

POET: I was born at these crossroads. Here all the paths were planned in advance. There are no chance encounters. To get away. Away from these roads of illusions. That's why I left. But ever since I've seen only coldness.

WOMAN: I never had the choice. I'm a woman. I was born to rupture.

POET (*to* PROMPTER): Her. Isn't she the woman? The flower-woman.

WOMAN: The escape-woman. The opium-woman.

POET (*still addressing* PROMPTER): The love-woman. The muse-woman.

WOMAN: The cow-woman. I was born with this weight. I was born . . .

POET: To give birth.

WOMAN: Never. (*silence*)

POET: I was born at the crossroads, here at the sacrificial site, where the victim was dragged, where the scapegoat was chased out into the desert.

(*Both the* WOMAN *and the* POET *grope for words. The* PROMPTER *stares absently into space.*)

WOMAN: I was born here, in this knot.

POET: In . . . this gap.

WOMAN: In . . . this unending . . .

POET: Unending . . .

PROMPTER (*coming to*): Explosion.

WOMAN: This knot, this gap, this unending explosion.

COP (*waking up*): I was born into order. And to maintain order, I'll pull apart, fix up, and flatten out.

WOMAN: So was I.

POET: I was born into order. But when I had to bend myself backwards to fit in, I understood. Something was missing in this order. Something like a counterorder.

COP (*throwing himself on the* POET): You little . . .

WOMAN (*intervening*): Six chances, remember. (*The* COP *drops the* POET *and goes back to lie on the bench.*)

PROMPTER: He was a stillborn child. But when he appeared the whole family applauded. A simple reflex. But the cry he let out at birth wasn't one of life, just survival.

POET: A little after my birth, I met the painter. I hid his forbidden pictures someplace where he helped me camouflage my censored dreams. (*He exits.*)

WOMAN: Coming around a bend, I met a philosopher one day. He was standing there, haranguing an imaginary crowd. "Where were you when the books were waiting to be read? When the speeches filled with lies were waiting to be silenced? The crumbling building demanded beams and stones. It got words, words, and good intentions, always the best of intentions. And sawdust and ashes. Perversion set in. One day man saw his ideal fall apart. He wasn't a man anymore. Searching, chasing, trying, rejecting, trying again. He got lost in the figures of his own calculations. Knowledge corrupted itself. It turned into indoctrination, blasphemy of the spirit. Where were you when the heroes who had vanquished the gods went to sit on the thrones, still warm. Here come our heroes. What are they saying? What are they predicting?"

Here comes the peddler with his bag of miracles. What is he selling? Ancestral masks, bits of colored glass turned dull and dusty, sunglasses for a sun that never appears. "Here comes the peddler. How much for these ancestral masks, for these clown masks? Ask for the latest invention, the surprise of the year, I named it the old age elixir and for the first hundred clients, a special gift, a trick mirror for luring birds. Get your tonic for premature aging, on sale at your authorized black market, at your local library and in children's bookstores, and in vending machines, get your old age tonic, your elixir of winter slumber, the balm that will close your eyes and turn them a deep pacific-paradise blue."

Scream. You want to scream. (*She opens her mouth in a scream but no sound emerges.*) But you mustn't scream. Someone will hear your voice in the night and come gag you. What do you do not to scream? You turn on the television and a chill runs down your spine. It's time for the petrification-drug commercial. You open the paper; it's full of slogans for the eternal sleeping pill that will mummify you. On all the walls, there are giant posters for trick mirrors, new and improved.

Cry. You want to cry. (*She begins to cry but stops suddenly.*) But you mustn't cry. What do you do not to cry? You laugh even if you don't feel like it. At all. (*She looks sad, then bursts out with a hysterical laugh. She stops abruptly.*) But you mustn't laugh either. Someone will hear you and will somehow know that you can't fake anything, not even sleep. (*Silence. The* POET *enters.*)

POET: After my friend died, I left. All I knew was leaving, find someplace else, something other than feeling stuck.

WOMAN: After my friend Rachel died . . .

POET: Rachel was born to die because her legs danced freely. They refused to march in step.

WOMAN: After the death of my friend, all I could do was stay, watch the walls crack and tumble on me, watch people I loved changing, into rags, into dead wood, into bewitched birds, into mad dogs.

POET: What else could I do? Stay here? Scream? Cry? Lie down and go to sleep?

COP (*in his sleep*): Sleep is peace.

POET: How can I be satisfied with sleep? With hypnosis, with suggested dreams?

WOMAN: You went away.

POET: What else could I do? Be like you, on those nights when your body swells against a thousand narrow walls? When you wander from one anonymous street corner to another selling what's left of your flesh, exchanging scraps of your body for scraps of gray bills. What could I have done? I shut myself away. (*He puts his hands over his ears. The* WOMAN *approaches and speaks to him. She moves her lips but there is no sound. The* PROMPTER *marks the time. The* POET *doesn't hear the* WOMAN. *She exits.*)

What could I have done? (*He begins to sing:*)

I dreamt of a body
A supple body
An open body
Delirious
I dreamt of a body.

(*He falls asleep. Music. A woman enters and dances.*
Blackout. Lights come back up.)

POET (*waking up*): Play your life for double or nothing,
that's what I should have done. Show your fist in the
street every evening you feel depressed. Grab the cop
by the skin of his neck and shout in his face: Zombie.
Zombie. Zombie. (*He grabs the* COP *and starts shaking
him. The* COP *continues to sleep.*)

COP (*in his sleep*): Sleep is peace.

POET (*like a boxing referee counting a knock-out*): One: hyp-
notized. Two: sterilized. Three: ostracized, Four . . .
(*The* COP *is beginning to wake up.*) And Ten: You're out.
(*The* COP *is awake.*) A knock-out. (*He steps on the* COP.)
Down, down, you bastard watch-dog.

COP: Is this show almost over? (*looking around*) Where
did she go?

POET: Good morning.

COP: Where is she?

POET: Granted, it's never morning here.

COP: Where did she go?

(*The* POET *points toward the wings. A pause.*)

COP: So you came back from far away.

POET: Very far away.

COP: Where exactly were you?

POET: Over there. Beyond the thousandth roadblock.

COP: What did you bring back with you? (*The* POET *takes out a flute and begins to play. The* COP *tries it but plays very badly. The* POET *holds his ears. They laugh.*)

POET: And what were you doing all that time?

COP: Maintaining law and order.

POET: I see.

COP: You know, arrests, conditioning, controlling the flow of . . .

POET: Blood? (*The* COP *grins.*) Your headband is stained. (*pause*) Why do you carry that club?

COP: The better to club you with, my boy.

POET: Why do you wear those leather boots?

COP: The better to kick your ass, my boy.

POET: And that uniform?

COP: The better to be recognized, my boy.

POET: Why is it the color of rust?

COP: Because I am hard as iron, my boy.

POET: And why is your head so square?

COP: That's just my style, my boy. (*pointing to the* POET's *hair*) And what's that stuff on your head?

POET: That's just my style, old man.

COP: What were you doing over there?

POET: Traveling.

COP: Suspect. (*more severe*) What else?

POET: I . . . well . . . I . . .

COP (*grabbing him*): You what?

POET: Artistically . . .

COP: Politically.

POET: The . . . (*The* COP *hits him with the club. He falls to the ground and the* COP *continues hitting him.*)

COP (*shouting*): Politically! (*counting like a referee*) One: outlaw. Two: pariah. Three: You're out.

THE CROSSROADS

(*The* POET *is lying like a corpse. The* WOMAN *is by his side. The* COP *stands at a distance, looking sheepish.*)

WOMAN (*to the* COP): You broke your promise.

COP: Sorry. Just a reflex . . . a . . .

PROMPTER: A conditioned reflex.

COP: Yeah, professional . . .

PROMPTER: Conditioning.

COP: Professional conditioning . . . (*He exits.*)

POET: If I make it, I'll go down deeper than sleep and I'll stay there.

WOMAN: Why did you come back?

POET: Because you were stuck in my skin like a splinter. I came back to cure myself of you.

WOMAN: So are you cured now?

POET: I love you. I don't know why I carry you around in my body. And my body has become more familiar since I breathed you. I don't know who you are. I know you so little, but I love you.

WOMAN: So badly.

POET: So strongly.

WOMAN: So dishonestly.

POET: How can you be so mysterious and yet have so much light in your eyes? I don't know what you can see in there nor what your body is smiling at. But I know it's something beyond the world and its fears. The world of deserts, the world of ruins, the world of cops. Far beyond. If I make it, I'll go as far as your gaze and I won't be afraid anymore. Never again. Have you suffered a lot too?

WOMAN: From the time of pain I borrowed the time to learn, to wait, to give. There was no time left for suffering. (*Silence.*)

POET (*turning away*): I had so much time, time to be alone.

WOMAN: Some nights when it was too white or too cold or too low, I'd walk to the road he had taken and I'd talk to myself . . .

POET: I talked to myself on my way.

WOMAN: I remembered when I was a child . . .

POET: I thought maybe I had been wrong too early . . . (*He continues to mouth words silently and to gesture as the* WOMAN *speaks.*)

WOMAN: I could have left too. Maybe with him. But he wouldn't have wanted me to come. Anyway, what's the sense in going up and down the paths you had no part in tracing. I could have left, turned in circles, from detour to detour, and then come back, the way he did. (*Similarly, she mouths words silently and gestures as the* POET *speaks.*)

POET: She would have preferred I stayed stuck here, that I'd burned my books, learned their language and buried my questions. I left. She didn't understand.

WOMAN: I understood. I understood because I'm a woman. I understood but much later. I'm a woman, this thing with roots. This thing grounded in the earth. This thing which changes into sons and daughters. If I don't find a way out of here, my children will also be born at these crossroads.

POET: I didn't want that. I wanted another time for those children, another road named the future.

WOMAN (*going to peer in the jar of water*): I want to see farther than the future, the future which is so close it burns your eyes. The only one offered me and the children I bear. A future that comes out of a past of lost and forgotten things, absences, lapses and relapses, falls, eclipses. A future is an empty time that you fill up with yourself. I want to fill the future with myself. I want to leave my footprints on time. Again. And again. Until time takes on my shape. That would be a future in measure with my present. Presence. The future is presence.

POET: The present has exhausted itself. Time has consumed itself at these crossroads.

WOMAN: I have to find a way out before dawn. A new morning. A new sun. I'd like to carry my roots far away.

POET: Time is running out.

WOMAN: I have to find a way through time. Because when the street light goes out and time stops, I'll be alone again. Looking for what? Hiding what? Saving what?

Poet (*laughing*): In a dead city I met a mad priest.

COP: Is it over yet?

POET: In a dead city I met a mad priest who was shouting alone in the sun: "Save your soul!"

COP: No one's ever told me anything like that. Save my soul. Day and night I hear: "Save your skin." I have to save my skin and my bones, my stomach and its bread and its excrements. Save my eyes by closing them, save my ears by plugging them with cotton, save my tongue by counting to ten before I speak, time to forget what you wanted to say.

WOMAN: The pleasure of the eyes is to see. The pleasure of the ears is to hear. The pleasure of the tongue is to ask why. Why? Why? It's a painful word. The pleasure of the body is to . . . is to . . .

PROMPTER: Don't forget Rachel.

COP: They just told me it was urgent to save my skin by locking it in this rigid armor. Save my body and its clotted blood. I'm frightened. It's fear that fills up my soul. I can't afford the luxury of an empty soul like you desperate, suffering, poetic, romantic junkies. I don't feel empty. I'm perfectly sure of what's there in the place of my soul. I can feel this thing which balances my body and gives me that assurance which you see as bravado, this martial bearing that you think is rigidity. I am full, satisfied. Full of fear. That thing that eats you alive until you don't feel anything at all. By the time it gets to your heart, you've already lost your head. You feel it in your stomach and it all gets knotted up in there. Only the excrement escapes. You feel it in your joints and your ligaments start tearing by the thousands. Just then you feel it in your balls and that's all that's left.

WOMAN: I'm scared.

COP: How do you save your soul? Nobody ever told me how.

WOMAN: I'm scared.

POET: She had happy legs. And then one day . . .

WOMAN: I'm scared.

COP: They told me blindness was the pleasure of the eyes . . . They taught me to plug my ears against the screams of the tortured.

WOMAN: I'm scared.

COP: They taught me to love only my own heart and I hardened it so it would never have to learn pain.

POET: About the time of pain . . .

WOMAN: I took the time to learn. And the time to hope.

POET: And the time to believe.

WOMAN: And the time to wait.

POET: And the time to forget.

COP: There are nights like this when I wish I could love something else. Crack open this heart. Some nights I would have felt so . . . felt so . . .

PROMPTER: Free. (*The street lamp goes out.*)

COP (*turning toward the* PROMPTER): No! (*The others turn and notice that the street lamp has gone out.*) Okay, it's over. It's day now. Curtain. (*No curtain falls. In a commanding voice*) Curtain! (*The* COP *grabs the* POET.)

WOMAN (*to the audience*): We can still gain some time. (*to* COP) It's only the intermission.

COP: Okay, I'll wait. (*He goes back to the bench*)

WOMAN: We have to do something. The light is out.

This intermission can't last forever. We have to do something. We have to go on.

PROMPTER: There's nothing more to say.

WOMAN: Do something.

PROMPTER: What?

WOMAN: Blow on the lamp. (*The* PROMPTER *hesitates a moment. She gestures insistently.*)

PROMPTER: Fire . . . fire . . . flame . . . flame . . . (*He gestures ceremonially while blowing words toward the lamp. The lamp does not go on. The* POET *is playing the flute.*)

WOMAN: I have to find a way out of this. If I don't, my children will never be born. Or they'll be born at the crossroads. More sons and daughters born into this rottenness and the cycle starts all over again.

PROMPTER: Fire . . . flame . . . embers . . . (*The lamp flickers.*)

WOMAN: I have to grow roots that will reach farther than the day the children will be born.

PROMPTER (*excited*): Flame . . . Embers . . . Lightning . . . (*The lamp flickers.*)

WOMAN: I need to find a way before dawn or my children will reincarnate swollen bodies, and licking original wounds, will be sacrificed at these crossroads for a sin never committed.

POET: Teach me to read the future.

WOMAN (*taking him by the hand and leading him to the water jar*): Centuries are swallowed up in this intermission without end. Look. There's a future going by, swallowed by the silence. There's another, pausing, moving on. Stubborn, it comes back again and is swallowed by indifference. And another . . . there are many futures.

POET: There are many futures.

PROMPTER: Lightning. Lightning. Light. (*The lamp lights up.*)

POET: Now what?

WOMAN: We have to do something.

PROMPTER: What? (*A pause.*)

WOMAN: The Cop. He's coming back. (*to* PROMPTER) Do something.

POET: I don't want to leave you again.

WOMAN: But you will. We always leave. Even if we love someone. Even if we've mastered each other like the lion and the tamer. Even if we wear each other's scars. You are alone. So am I.

THE CROSSROADS

POET: It hurts.

WOMAN: I know.

POET: This feeling it's starting all over again.

WOMAN: When you question memory, the answer is like a gash.

POET: You think about things that were misplaced, forgotten or dead, left far behind.

WOMAN: That's what hurts. What you leave behind. Don't leave me in your past when you go away. I wouldn't know how to get out to wait for you a little further on. If you wait for me just beyond where you are, you won't feel the pain.

POET: I'll be waiting . . . but I'll still feel the pain.

WOMAN: There are many futures. We'll meet again. Tell me we'll meet again.

POET (*smiling*): We'll meet again.

WOMAN: Keep that smile when you leave here. It will help you forget me.

POET: I don't want to forget you.

WOMAN: I don't want to be a memory. I don't want to be what you already lost. But your hope, your plans.

(*The* COP *seizes the* POET *and begins to drag him away.*)

POET: Why? Why?

WOMAN: For your being everything that will amaze you . . . Why did you come back?

POET: I was haunted by your shadow no matter how much I tried to kill you in my mind.

WOMAN: Don't say anything about love. It's bad luck to call things by their sacred names. (*pause*) There are many futures.

POET: We'll meet again?

PROMPTER: Enough. Enough. (*The three actors freeze during the following tirade.*) Twenty years this has been going on, twenty years of starting over, again and again. Every evening the same play runs through my mind, the same image of actors putting on the mask, the costume, the emotions of characters. Characters. But this isn't about characters. It's about me. I am the Poet. This story playing in my mind is my history.

Twenty years in the dark, in this prison where everything disappears. Where only memory remains. Repetitive, crazed, careless memory that I keep goading, prompting, whispering it words and pictures to save them from forgetfulness.

Henceforth I am only memory. That's been my only means of existence ever since I was given a box of matches and a script written in my own hand. A double turn of the key and everything is settled for eternity. My words, my words . . . my gestures were convulsive but my words . . . I believed in them a long time ago, in their power to reduce pain to its essence, to a strict minimum . . . and to compensate for absence with illusion.

Memory. Yes, memory is needed for all the vanishing species of mankind. The poet . . . disappeared. The traveler . . . disappeared. The painter . . . disappeared. The philosophers . . . disappeared. The priest . . . disappeared. The woman . . . disappeared. The child . . . disappeared. Who's next? But there's no one left. Whose turn?

This evening I'd like to stop it all there. Rid my mind of these obsessive memories. Stop everything. Escape. Leave before it's too late, before you, the last surviving species, disappear. Get out. I know the ending, it's always the same. The end, the end, the end . . .

Senouvo Agbota Zinsou

YEVI'S ADVENTURES
IN MONSTERLAND

Translated from the French
by Danielle C. Brunon

Sénouvo Agbota Zinsou was born in Lomé, Togo, in 1946. He continued his studies in France, receiving degrees in theater and communications. In 1968 he co-founded a university theater company, after working with several student companies, and began to be known outside Togo when his play *On joue la comédie* received first prize in Radio France Internationale's 1972 Inter-African Theater Competition. As part of the 1977 Festival of Black Arts and Culture in Lagos, Nigeria, he directed a production of the same play which later toured France. Since 1978, Zinsou has been director of the Troupe Nationale du Togo, a theater, ballet and music company. He directs the company in productions of his own plays, including *L'Arc en ciel* and *Le Club*. Zinsou premiered *La tortue qui chante* (*The Singing Tortoise*) in 1986 during the Francophone Summit in Lomé in a production that was later performed in France at the 1987 Limoges Festival. Zinsou is also a prizewinning short story writer, whose fiction and plays are published in France by Hatier.

Danielle Brunon was Assistant to the Artistic Director of Ubu Repertory Theater from 1984 to 1986 and Coordinator of Ubu's 1987 Festival of New Plays from French-speaking Africa. In 1986 she directed a reading of Jean-Claude Grumberg's *On Vacation* at Ubu Repertory Theater. She also adopted and translated Diderot's *La Religieuse* and is the co-translator of Denise Chalem's *The Sea Between Us* published by Ubu Repertory Theater Publications. She presently lives and works in Paris.

The premiere of the English translation of *Yevi's Adventures in Monsterland* was directed by Michi Jones at the David and Rae Aronow Theater at the City College of New York as part of the 1988 Ubu International Festival on March 17, 1988.

CHARACTERS

YEVI
THE STORYTELLER
THE GIANT
THE ALMIGHTY
THE MONSTERS
SADOMONSTER
SWEETMONSTER
GIGGLYMONSTER
THE SHEEP

STORYTELLER: So, you've heard of Yevi and I don't have to introduce him to you. Watch it now, don't you go mistaking him for one of those common little spiders that lurk in any nook and cranny. No! He is an important person.

YEVI (*rushing in*): Hey? Who said I'm not important? Eh? Who said it? I'm in every single story.

STORYTELLER: Sure. Cool it, Yevi, cool it.

YEVI: I want to know who said I'm not important.

STORYTELLER: No one did, Sir Yevi, no one. Cool it, Yevi.

YEVI: Everyone is talking about me. Everywhere. Am I right?

STORYTELLER: Yes, Yevi, you are.

YEVI: Bedtime stories on the radio: I'm in them all, am I not?

STORYTELLER: Yes sir, Yevi, you are.

YEVI: Who do storytellers tell stories about, in every village, in every town?

STORYTELLER: About you, Mr. Yevi, nobody but you.

YEVI: Well then? (*pause*) Even on TV, even a TV crew came to film me the other day in a story the children produced for the school play. And the Inspector was present, the Inspector himself, do you hear?

STORYTELLER: As a matter of fact, sir, that is precisely the story we wish to present to our lovely audience tonight. So, Sir Yevi, would you be so kind as to remind us of its title.

YEVI: Naturally, you mean "Yevi's - that's me - Latest Adventures in Monsterland."

STORYTELLER: Yes. Music, please, for the parade of characters.

SCENE 1

STORYTELLER (*to* YEVI): So, my friend. Where do you think it's going to get you to go around bragging like you just did in that bit just now?

YEVI: That bit! It worked didn't it? I got applause. Great applause. Huge applause. I even got a standing ovation!

STORYTELLER: Fine. But after all . . .

YEVI: After all what? You mean I'm hungry?

STORYTELLER: I didn't say that . . . The point is, you're really hungry. I mean you're starving.

YEVI: So what? I'm not the only one who's starving here, I'm not the only one who's hard hit by the famine, everyone in the village is, everyone, including you.

STORYTELLER: True. But do you know what the difference is between you and me? Between you and everyone else?

YEVI: Yes I do. I most certainly, certainly do.

STORYTELLER: Oh, you do? What is it then?

YEVI: The difference is, that unlike everyone else, I am an important person, renowned, famous, prestigious.

STORYTELLER: No, my friend no. The difference is, Yevi, that not only are you starving like everyone else, but on top of it all, you are a jerk!

YEVI: Me? A jerk?

STORYTELLER: That's right. Because you just have to waste the tiny bit of energy you've got left in your muscles, and the tiny bit of air you've got left in your lungs to go around bragging all the time.

YEVI: That's an insult. I won't forgive that. You're going to get it. (*He makes a fist, bulges his chest, and chases the* STORYTELLER *around.* The STORYTELLER *exits.* YEVI *is left out of breath.*) Oh! He . . . He . . . got away . . . got away . . . But I'll get him . . . soon . . . Oh! My feet hurt . . .Ow! My knees hurt . . . my back . . . Oh! I get it: I'm hungry. I'm even hungrier now. Ow! My stomach! My stomach's almost disappeared. I'm really hungry! (*yelling*) I'm hungry! I'm hungry.

(*Enter a* GIANT *who is twelve feet tall.* YEVI *sees him.*)

THE GIANT: Who shouted? Who shouted, I'm hungry? Was it you, little bug? Who shouted?

YEVI (*trembling*): No . . . No . . .

GIANT: If you're lying I'll crush you under my thumb.

YEVI: Yes . . . Yes . . .

GIANT: And why are you hungry?

YEVI: I haven't eaten for two . . . three days . . .

GIANT: What do you mean, you haven't eaten for two, three days? If you're lying I'll crush you under my thumb.

YEVI: Oh! sir, I did eat, I did eat.

GIANT: When?

YEVI: I just did.

GIANT: What do you mean you just ate and you're yelling "I'm hungry." If you're lying . . .

YEVI: I ate, I ate . . . I just finished my meal.

GIANT: What do you mean, "meal"?

YEVI: I've eaten, I haven't eaten . . . I'm hungry, not hungry . . . Whatever you say, sir.

GIANT (*laughing*): Ha ha ha little bug. You don't know what you're talking about.

YEVI: Actually, the fact is, sir, that when faced with your size . . . your strength . . . you who make the earth tremble when you walk, who make rocks tumble when you laugh . . .

GIANT: Enough! When you're hungry do not speak.

YEVI: Yes, sir.

GIANT: When you're hungry do not shout.

YEVI: Yes, sir.

GIANT: When you're hungry do not run.

YEVI: Yes, sir.

GIANT: When you're hungry do not eat.

YEVI: Yes, sir.

GIANT: Ha ha ha. Bye bye, little bug. (*He leaves.*)

YEVI: Please, sir, please, big brother, uncle, cousin, Grandpa . . .

GIANT (*menacing, turning around*): What?

YEVI: Nothing, sir. Goodbye, sir.

GIANT (*laughing*): Ha ha ha!

YEVI: But . . . sir . . . Uncle . . .

GIANT (*menacing, turning around*): What?

YEVI: Nothing, sir . . . Goodbye, sir . . .

Giant (*laughing*): Ha ha ha!

YEVI: Sir, a piece of . . . manioc bread?

GIANT: What?

YEVI: Nothing, sir . . . Goodbye, sir.

(*The* GIANT *exits, laughing. Enter the* STORYTELLER.)

STORYTELLER: You are stupid, you are so stupid!

YEVI: No way, you're stupid.

STORYTELLER (*menacing*): What?

YEVI: I mean stu . . . storyteller.

STORYTELLER: Aha! That's more like it. But you could have asked that man where to find something to eat.

YEVI: How does he know? I was just about to ask him, and then I figured he probably didn't know.

STORYTELLER: What do you mean, he didn't know? You see this man. He is tall, big and fat and you figure he doesn't know where to find food? Now, is that smart?

YEVI: In other words, if a man is tall, big and fat that means he must know where to find food.

STORYTELLER: Naturally . . . Look. Why are we so short and skinny? Because we don't know where to find food.

YEVI: But . . . What do we do now that he's gone?

STORYTELLER: You jerk. That man's feet are as big as canoes, and his footsteps are easy to find.

YEVI: That's it. Let's go and follow him right away.

STORYTELLER: No, you jerk!

YEVI: No way! You're the jerk. I'm not going to let you insult me all the time.

STORYTELLER: If you don't want me to insult you all the time, then you ought to try being a little smarter. You want to follow this man whose nostrils are as big as a well: he'll smell you in the air, he'll turn around, and even if you're ten miles away, he'll see you, run after you, stretch out his arm which is longer than ten palm trees all lined up, he'll catch you and crush you under his thumb which is bigger than a boulder. So, is that smart? To let yourself get crushed by a thumb bigger than a boulder?

YEVI: No, but then . . .

STORYTELLER: So, we've got to wait. Let a day or two go by.

YEVI: Two days? I'll have starved to death by then.

STORYTELLER: My dear, one must be patient and persevering to survive. We have to wait at least one day. Meanwhile, I'll find out how we can get to that giant's country without getting ourselves crushed by a thumb bigger than a boulder.

YEVI (*sad*): All right. If I'm not dead by then.

STORYTELLER: Listen, if you want to feel less hungry, get some sleep: go to bed and go to sleep. Goodnight.

(*He exits.* YEVI *lies down, closes his eyes for a little while, then gets up.*)

YEVI: It's stupid! It's stupid to go to bed when you're hungry. You can't get to sleep. (*He imitates the* GIANT.) When you're hungry, do not go to bed. Yes, sir. When you're hungry, do not go to sleep. Yes, sir. Yes, sir. What, yes sir? Yes, sir. (*pause*) Oh! It's a pain, it's a real pain to have to wait a whole day to eat when you're hungry. Isn't there a way to speed time up? Hey! I know! I'll light a bonfire right in front of that stupid storyteller's house, to make him think the sun is rising already. (*He goes to light the fire and starts yelling.*) My friend! My dear friend! It's morning, it's morning! (*The* STORYTELLER *enters, rubbing his eyes, having just woken up.*)

STORYTELLER: It's daytime all right. (*He notices the fire.*) But . . . Yevi, you're a jerk. You would think of lighting a fire. Let me sleep. (*He exits.*)

YEVI (*alone again*): It's stupid. What can I do to make time go faster? Oh! I know. I'll crow like a rooster. (*He imitates the rooster.*) Cock-a-doodle-doo!

STORYTELLER: What is it? What's wrong?

YEVI: Nothing, sir.

STORYTELLER: If nothing's wrong, then why are you yelling?

YEVI: But . . . I'm not the one who's yelling.

STORYTELLER: Then, who is?

YEVI: Well . . . It's the rooster crowing.

STORYTELLER: What rooster? Well, that rooster's a real jerk.

YEVI: What? Are you insulting me again?

STORYTELLER: So you're the rooster?

YEVI: No, I'm not, but . . .

STORYTELLER: But you're the jerk?

YEVI: I am definitely not, not at all. I'm neither a jerk, nor a rooster . . .

STORYTELLER: If you're neither a rooster, nor a jerk, go to bed. It isn't morning, yet. (*He exits.*)

YEVI: Oh! That stupid storyteller! What other plot can I make up to make him think it's morning? Eh? (*Pause. He becomes nervous, agitated.*) But it's really terrible that it takes so long for morning to come when you're hungry. And what if I die before sunrise? Eh? That whole pile of food in store! And I die! Who's going to eat it all, huh? Everyone else: uncles, aunts, cousins, nephews, with their aunts, uncles, cousins . . . I know those gluttons: they'll have a fancy funeral, they'll eat for seven days on end: lamb, beef, chicken, goat . . . Gboma, ademe, fetrima, vegetable sauces. All of it, and I'll have starved to death. Now, is that smart? And they'll drink: deha palm wine, millet Tchoukoutou beer, sodabi palm tree liquor, and gin and whisky, that white man's beer. All of it! They'll be merry, sing and dance, sweat, stagger and fall. And I, I will have starved to death. Is that smart? Oh! I'm talking too much. When you're hungry you don't talk. I'd better try to find a way to make the sun rise instead. Hey! I know when the sun rises, the women go and fetch water at the creek. On the way they chat, giggle, bicker and the noise of their pots and pans is enough to wake up the whole village. I'll pretend I'm them. (*He gathers pots and pans and hits them against each other, adopting various different female voices.*) Hello, Kossiwa. Hello Afi. Did you sleep well? Yes. And the children? Yes. And your husband? Yes. Your uncle? Yes. Your father? Yes. The other day you promised you . . . Hey Adjoa! The other day you took my pan. What? I took your pan? You took my bucket! (*He hits the pans against each others.*) Pow Pow Pow. You thief! You liar!

Break it up! Stop hitting each other. You scratched me You gave me a black eye! My tooth got knocked out; I'm going to bite you. I'm going to tear you in two. *Òbóbóbóbóééé![1]* Adjoa is dying! Afi is a witch!

(*The* STORYTELLER *has been watching the scene for a long time but* YEVI *has not noticed. He tries to hold back a fit of laughter but can no longer resist.*)

STORYTELLER: Ha ha ha. Yevi, you're going crazy.

YEVI: Yes, I have gone crazy. But how can I help it when I'm so hungry?

STORYTELLER: You're hungry and you're screaming. You're getting yourself all worked up. You're beating yourself up and arguing with yourself. Now is that very intelligent?

YEVI: What am I supposed to do to make tomorrow come quickly?

STORYTELLER: Be patient, until daybreak.

YEVI: Be patient? And what if I die before daybreak? Huh?

STORYTELLER: Well then, I'll call your uncles, your cousins, your nephews, your whole village and your relatives from other villages, and they'll all bury you.

YEVI: They'll bury me and they'll eat all that food. They'll drink, they'll dance, sing, stagger and fall. And I'll have starved to death. That's really smart. After they bury me, when they've eaten, drunk, danced and on and on, then they will bury my hair and my nails to have another chance to eat, drink and dance some more. And I'll have starved to death. That's really smart. After burying my hair, and my nails, then they'll finish mourning and celebrate to have a third occasion to eat drink and dance at my expense. And I'll have starved to death. That's really smart. When they finish mourning they'll still cele-brate the first, second, third, up to the one hundredth anniversary of my death so they can eat, drink and dance a hundred times, still at my expense. And me, I'll have starved to death. Is that smart?

STORYTELLER: Listen, Yevi. When you're hungry you don't get philosophical. I'm going to bed to get some sleep. (*He exits.*)

YEVI: That guy is mean. He doesn't want me to go eat with him. Fortunately, I'm smarter than he is. I'm going to put ashes in his bag and make a hole in it. That way, when he leaves, the ashes will fall along the way and I'll be able to follow him. (*He exits.*)

STORYTELLER (*entering*): Finally, that jerk Yevi has gone to bed. While he's asleep, I'm going to sneak away. I don't want him to come with me. It's dangerous to have a companion who is such an impatient and indiscreet fool. He could get me into trouble. Still, I'll bring a little bit of food back for him so he doesn't starve to death. (*He takes his bag, hangs it over his shoulder and exits. Enter YEVI.*)

YEVI: That guy is really too stupid. He took his bag and put it over his shoulder without even noticing that I put a hole and some ashes in it. I'm going to follow him. (*He starts walking on the trail of ashes, step by step.*) All that food to look forward to! Lamb, beef, goat, chicken! I'll eat part of it on the spot, I'll salt part of it, I'll smoke part of it, and when I've had enough, I'll sell part of it, and get rich. I'll buy really fancy houses with velvet rugs, shiny and sumptuous furniture, air conditioners, television, stereo system . . . You say that doesn't suit me? Well, let me tell you that I, Yevi, have a right to luxury and comfort like everybody else. I have a right to get rich, to have cars, coconut plantations, palm tree plantations, cattle . . . (*He walks a little way without realizing that he has lost track of the trail of ashes. Suddenly he comes back to reality.*) Where's the trail of ashes? I lost it? I'm lost! That mean storyteller must have noticed the ashes and the hole I put in the bag. So he dumped the ashes and now he's going to eat all that food by himself. And I'll starve to death. Is that smart? Fortunately, I'm smarter than he is. I'm going to scream . . . (*Enter the* STORYTELLER *suddenly. He covers* YEVI's *mouth with his hand.*)

STORYTELLER: Don't scream, stupid!

YEVI: No, let me scream!

STORYTELLER: The monsters will hear you and . . .

YEVI: I don't give a damn, let me scream.

STORYTELLER: They'll come and crush us . . .

YEVI: Too bad, I want to scream . . .

STORYTELLER: They'll crush us under their thumbs bigger than boulders . . .

YEVI: I said: I don't give a damn and I'm going to scream.

STORYTELLER: Fine. I've got a charm to become invisible as soon as the monsters appear. So go ahead and scream. When they come they'll see no one but you. Scream!

YEVI: Is it true that you have a charm.

STORYTELLER: I wouldn't give it to you anyway. Scream.

YEVI: You should have told me that . . .

STORYTELLER: I have nothing to tell you. Scream.

YEVI: But . . .

STORYTELLER: No "buts." Scream!

YEVI: I beg of you . . .

STORYTELLER: I beg of you: scream.

YEVI: I kneel before you.

STORYTELLER: So do I. Scream.

YEVI: I'm sorry. Let's not keep on playing this game when we're so hungry. Those nasty monsters will eat all that food all by themselves and we'll have starved to death. Now is that smart?

STORYTELLER: All right. That's enough. Promise that from now on, you will be discreet as an ant on top of a mountain, that you will not speak at all . . .

YEVI: I promise.

STORYTELLER: That you will make no comments, no observations about the monsters when you see them. . . .

YEVI: I promise.

STORYTELLER: That you will not utter so much as a sound!

YEVI: I promise.

STORYTELLER: Here you are, then! Here is the charm to make you invisible. But if you utter a sound and the monsters hear you . . .

YEVI: Not a chance!

STORYTELLER: They have a counter-charm that allows them to see the invisible . . .

YEVI: Really?

STORYTELLER: They'll use it.

YEVI: Let's hope they don't use it!

STORYTELLER: They'll see you.

YEVI: Let's hope they don't see me!

STORYTELLER: They'll catch you.

YEVI: No! No!

STORYTELLER: They'll crush you.

YEVI: No! No! Let's especially hope they don't crush me!

STORYTELLER: So be quiet.

YEVI: I'm quiet.

STORYTELLER: If you keep on blabbering I'll take the charm back.

YEVI: All right, I'm quiet.

STORYTELLER: Come along. We'll wait over here.

YEVI: But why do we have to wait again? I'm hungry.

STORYTELLER: Jerk! The monsters are coming to dine at a kind of reception. First their servants arrive, and arrange the tables, the chairs and the settings. Then the guests begin to arrive in hierarchical order: from the shortest to the tallest. Wait and see. Be quiet. It's time. Look.

YEVI (*seeing the* MONSTERS *arrive*): Look! They each have two heads! Well I never! Double-headed people!

STORYTELLER: They're the servants. But don't yell so loud.

YEVI: Look! Here are the monsters with three . . .

four . . . five . . . six heads! It's unbelievable! Wow, it's crowded. They're getting restless. They're really making a lot of noise.

STORYTELLER: Be quiet, Yevi. They're restless because they're getting ready for the entrance of their great leader. That one has seven heads. That makes him the Almighty.

YEVI: The Almighty? But the Almighty's God.

STORYTELLER: Be quiet. There is no God in Monsterland. Their God is the Almighty.

YEVI: Well, yes, that's exactly what I'm saying: their Almighty, that's God.

STORYTELLER: Not exactly. Their God: that's the Almighty.

YEVI: But it's the same thing.

STORYTELLER: Stop arguing, or else . . .

YEVI (*screaming*): There's the Almighty! There he is, the Almighty!

STORYTELLER: Be quiet!

YEVI: He's going to sit down . . .

STORYTELLER: Be quiet.

YEVI: The others are sitting after him.

STORYTELLER: Shut up! Or I'll take the charm back.

YEVI: All right! I'm quiet.

STORYTELLER: Now let's go. We're going to slip ourselves, invisible, under their tables and gather the crumbs.

YEVI: The crumbs! Why just the crumbs?

STORYTELLER: Stupid! Do you know what a crumb from these monsters is like? It's a piece as big as a person.

YEVI: Terrific! Pieces of food as big as people, and those are just the crumbs! Wow! I'm going right under the Almighty's table!

STORYTELLER: Shut up, stupid! Let's go. (*They exit.*)

SCENE 2

(The multi-headed MONSTERS *are seated, in order of height, while the seven-headed* ALMIGHTY *monster towers over everyone. They eat, drink and converse in an atmosphere of orgiastic excess.* YEVI *is right under the* ALMIGHTY'S *table. The* STORYTELLER, *who is a little farther away, under the table of a mere three-headed monster, often signals to* YEVI *to be quiet and careful. Both eat the crumbs and when they have had enough, they begin to fill their bags with them.* YEVI *tickles the* ALMIGHTY'S *foot.)*

THE ALMIGHTY (*thundering*): Ah! Something tickled my foot.

ALL THE SIX-HEADED MONSTERS: Something tickled the Almighty's foot!

ALL THE SIX AND FIVE-HEADED MONSTERS (*in unison*): Something tickled the Almighty's foot!

ALL THE SIX- FIVE- AND FOUR-HEADED MONSTERS: Something tickled the Almighty's foot!

ALL THE SIX- FIVE- FOUR- AND THREE-HEADED MONSTERS: Something tickled the Almighty's foot!

THE ALMIGHTY: Look for this thing!

(The MONSTERS, *except the* ALMIGHTY, *of course, start running around in all directions, getting very agitated and looking very angry.)*

THE ALMIGHTY (*laughing*): Ha ha ha. (*All the other*

MONSTERS *start laughing as well. The orchestrated laughter gets louder progressively, from the six-headed* MON-STERS, *down to the two-headed* MONSTERS.)

THE ALMIGHTY: Relax. I just wanted to test your devotion to me. (*laughing*) Ha ha ha. But, tell me. If something were to tickle my foot, what would you do? Well? You, six-headed Sadomonster, what would you do?

SADOMONSTER: I, six-headed Sadomonster, would capture this thing, and I would tear it up, bit by bit, bleed it, and fry it in boiling oil.

THE ALMIGHTY: You're too sadistic, Sadomonster!

YEVI (*whispering to the* STORYTELLER): Wow! That guy's really nasty!

STORYTELLER: Sh! Sh!

THE ALMIGHTY: I think someone whispered under my table.

ALL THE MONSTERS (*in order*): What Almighty Master?

THE ALMIGHTY (*laughing*): Ha ha ha. Nothing, calm down. That was to test how well you watch over my August Personage. But if someone were to whisper under my table, what would you do, two-headed Sweetmonster?

SWEETMONSTER: Well I, two-headed Sweetmonster,

would tell your Almighty Majesty that the person who is whispering under your table is a poor guy who is hungry and I would therefore entreat your Majesty to call upon this person, allow him to sit by your side, and serve him something to eat.

YEVI (*clapping*): Bravo! Bravo! Bravo! Sweetmonster!

THE ALMIGHTY (*frowning*): Who said "Bravo!" (*The question is repeated among the* MONSTERS. *Silence. The* ALMIGHTY *gets mad.*) Cowards! You're all nothing but cowards. One of you just said "Bravo!" and even went so far as to clap. And when I ask you who said "Bravo!", you're all silent. Bunch of cowards! I'm angry! I don't like being angry. I like to be happy. Where is three-headed Gigglymonster?

GIGGLYMONSTER: Here I am, Almighty Sir.

THE ALMIGHTY: Well then, find a story or a game to make us laugh.

(*He laughs and all the others imitate him in size order.*)

GIGGLYMONSTER: Almighty Lord, I have never ceased to think of means and ways by which I could entertain your August Personage. And I have found a very amusing game in which your August Personage can indulge during leisure time and mealtime, indeed I do say leisure time and mealtime, as eating has always been a game for your August Personage, has it not?

THE ALMIGHTY (*stupidly*): Yes. (*The yes is repeated in size order.*)

301

GIGGLYMONSTER: Then this is the way the game is played: when you eat, you eat, you eat, you eat until you're full, and when you don't know what else to do with that mountain of leftover food, well then, you get undressed. (*The other* MONSTERS *begin to laugh.*) Oh! No, no, no. Don't laugh. This is serious. So, you get undressed, you stand up on your chair, head down, bottoms up, butt in the air you take the food, toss it up, let it fall and catch it in your rear end! (*laughter*) Calm down, calm down. I haven't finished. Thus, the food, which normally enters through the mouth, now enters through the rear. (*laughter*)

THE ALMIGHTY: Terrific! (*repeated among the* MONSTERS) Let's give this game a try! Let's go. At my command! Heads down, bottoms up, take the food and Whee, Woooo! (*laughter*)

YEVI (*under the table*): Terrific! Terrific! Now there's so much food falling I don't know what to do with it all . . . but, but they're running out of meat. (*He loses hold of himself and yells.*) Almighty Sir, you're running out of meat! (*The* ALMIGHTY *becomes serious again.*)

THE ALMIGHTY: This time I'm sure someone spoke under my table. He even yelled. He must have a charm to make him invisible because I can't see anyone. Put on the counter-charm and find him. (*The* MONSTERS *put their counter-charm glasses on and start searching under the* ALMIGHTY's *table. While the* STORY-TELLER *manages to escape, unnoticed,* YEVI *is captured.*)

YEVI (*incessantly repeating*): Oh uncles, my dear uncles!

The Almighty: Since when have I become your uncle, you vile little bug?

The Monsters (*in size order*): Since when have we become your uncles, you vile little bug?

The Almighty: You're bugging me.

The Monsters: You're bugging the Almighty.

The Almighty: Six-headed Sadomonster!

Six-Headed Sadomonster: Here I am, Almighty Sir.

The Almighty: I hand him over to you. Do with him what you will.

Sadomonster: Thank you, Almighty Sir. I'll just give him a little present . . . What will it be? I could punch you . . .

Yevi (*trembling*): No, no, no, my uncle. You can't do that.

Sadomonster: Well then, I could kick you.

Yevi: No, no, my uncle. You'd crush me. I've just eaten. I haven't digested yet. I would do . . . dooo . . . dooo.

Sadomonster: If you do, I'll make you swallow it!

Yevi: Oh, my uncle!

SADOMONSTER: Ha ha ha! You're pathetic. All right, I won't kill you. Not right away at least. We're not mean, right? I'll give you a nice present instead. How about a pretty pearl necklace around your nice little neck?

YEVI: Are you serious, my uncle?

SADOMONSTER: I'm always serious, my nephew. The proof is, look, I'll put this on you right now. (*He puts the necklace on.*) There, you can go now. Goodbye, my "nephew."

YEVI (*very surprised*): Are you ser. . . .

SADOMONSTER (*thundering*): I'm always serious. Now get out!

YEVI (*excited, very happy*): Thank you, my uncle! You're so nice, my uncle! Goodbye to all of you, uncles. Goodbye my uncle the Almighty . . . (*He exits thanking them all. The* MONSTERS *burst out laughing as soon as he is gone.*)

SADOMONSTER: The viper says that children do not know death. He doesn't know that necklace makes him a slave and entirely dependent on me. Wherever he is, whatever he is doing, all I have to do is call my necklace and the necklace pulls him towards me uncontrollably. If he's lucky enough to meet someone within seven days who is stupider than he is, then he can escape by giving away the necklace. But I doubt it because that guy is really stupid. (*All the* MONSTERS *laugh.*)

SCENE 3

(YEVI *is alone on stage.*)

YEVI: That Sadomonster is a real jerk!

STORYTELLER (*entering*): You're back Yevi.

YEVI (*bragging*): Yes, here I am, in flesh and blood. Fortunately, I am smart, smarter than you are! Smarter than all those stupid monsters. They are such jerks. I eat their food, I tickle the Almighty jerk's foot, I make fun of them and when they catch me . . . guess what they do to me?

STORYTELLER: It's not hard to figure out: they give you the necklace of slavery.

YEVI (*stunned*): The necklace of slavery?

SADOMONSTER (*offstage*): My necklace! (*Uncontrollably,* YEVI *runs towards the voice.*)

STORYTELLER (*alone*): Poor Yevi. He didn't get it. But I do like him. I have to find a way to rescue him. But where can I find someone who is stupider than him?

YEVI (*out of breath, returns*): They made me run . . . run . . . run . . . I'm thirsty. Give me a little water . . . Something to drink. (*The* STORYTELLER *brings him water in a gourd but just as* YEVI *is about to take the gourd* . . .)

SADOMONSTER (*offstage*): My necklace! (YEVI *starts running again.*)

STORYTELLER: It's so sad. Now I see that after food, what man needs most is his freedom. The problem now is finding a way to restore Yevi's freedom. Otherwise he'll never be happy again. (YEVI *returns, more out of breath.*)

YEVI: Oh! Oh! . . . Please . . . Quickly . . . Give me water before he calls me again . . .

SADOMONSTER: (*offstage, thundering*): My necklace! (YEVI *runs.*)

STORYTELLER: I'm trying to figure out what brought on Yevi's ruin. First, his greed: why did he have to go right under the Almighty's table when he could have gotten a decent meal under any other smaller monster's table? (YEVI *returns, even more tired.*)

YEVI: I think . . . I'm dying . . . Quick, water . . .

SADOMONSTER (*offstage*): My necklace! (YEVI *runs.*)

STORYTELLER: The second thing that got my friend Yevi into trouble is his irresponsible, his completely happy-go-lucky personality. He thinks everything is a game, including his own life. What's the big idea to go and tickle the Almighty's foot?

(YEVI *returns, practically dead of exhaustion. He can no longer speak and can only signal for the water, panting. The* STORYTELLER *is about to give him a drink when the voice is heard again.* YEVI *runs.*)

STORYTELLER: The third thing that caused Yevi's mis-
fortune is his indiscretion. I tried to warn him. (*A
sheep goes by*.) That's it! A sheep! This might be the way
to rescue Yevi, because I do think the sheep is even
more stupid than Yevi. I'm not sure, but it's worth a
try. (*to the* SHEEP) Mister Sheep?

THE SHEEP: Yes sir.

STORYTELLER: I would like to give you a present because
I like you.

THE SHEEP: A present? What do you mean?

STORYTELLER: A pearl necklace one of my friends is
picking up for me. With that necklace, you'd be the
most beautiful sheep in the world.

THE SHEEP: The most beautiful sheep in the world? I
wouldn't mind at all.

STORYTELLER: The only thing is you'll have to grab the
necklace very quickly, when my friend gets here
because he's a . . . very busy guy, and he could run
off with the necklace. Then you wouldn't have it, and
you wouldn't be the most beautiful sheep in the world.

THE SHEEP: Oh! No! I must be the most beautiful sheep
in the world! Fortunately, I'm very smart. I'll manage.

(YEVI *enters, exhausted, and faints. The* SHEEP *jumps on
him, tears the necklace off.*)

SADOMONSTER (*offstage*): My necklace, my necklace!

(*The* SHEEP *runs.* YEVI *is saved. The* STORYTELLER *brings him water. He drinks, and regains consciousness. He stands up.*)

YEVI: Oh! I'm safe! I got rid of the necklace. Fortunately I'm smarter than . . .

STORYTELLER: Yes, smarter. Rather not as stupid as the sheep who took the necklace. Do you know what betrayed him? His vanity.

YEVI: That's his problem. (*He wants to leave but the* STORYTELLER *grabs him by his shirt.*)

STORYTELLER: Hey, wait a minute. You'd survive all these dangers without learning the moral of the story? Is that smart?

YEVI: Oh, to hell with the moral of the story. (*He leaves.*) I'm so exhausted I've got only one thing on my mind: I've got to get something to eat. (*He exits.*)

STORYTELLER: The storyteller in my village always had these words of wisdom: "Never get a fool out of trouble, he won't even notice.

Translator's Note:

[1] Cry of distress commonly used in many regions of Togo as a warning or call to nearby individuals and communities whenever something unusual or threatening is detected. The cry is uttered while bringing a hand up to the mouth and tapping it vehemently for resonance.